Through the Fires: Women in War

Narratives of Displaced Women in Gaza

Edited and Annotated by

Nawal Halawa

ISBN:979-8-9992568-3-6

LOC Preregistration Case # 1-14966527341

Cover Illustration by Hanadi Bader

Sligo Creek Publishing
9039 Sligo Creek Parkway
Silver Spring, Maryland 20901
https://www.sligocreekpublishing.com/

Introduction

The Palestinian woman in Gaza is not merely a witness to war; she stands at the heart of resistance. A resistance that does not carry weapons, but instead carries strength within her heart. It begins with a simple meal cooked over firewood, passes through long nights filled with fear and cold, and ends with the laughter of a child who has narrowly escaped death.

In Gaza, where there is no room for rest or safety, women transform into pillars of fire and light. Fire to ignite cooking flames, and light born from their courage and patience. They turn darkness into glimmers of life, despair into determination, and tears into resilience.

During the war, women were not just victims. They clung to wounds, carried their children while running under bombardment, preserved schoolbooks amidst the rubble of their homes, and stood in bread lines with the dignity of warriors.

With the patience of prophets, they endured hunger, and with the steadfastness of mountains, they bore displacement.

They slept on the ground, covered their children with their only garment.

Carried their homes on their shoulders, rebuilding them with love rather than cement. Every meal prepared from almost nothing was a victory.

Every candle lit so a child could study became a beacon of light in the tunnel of occupation.

This is the resistance that does not appear in news bulletins.

It wears no military rank, yet it carries the homeland in its heart and shelters it in prayer.

The women of Gaza are the invisible force keeping this nation alive.

They are heroines of a different kind names not written in battle reports, yet every surviving home, every smiling child, and every resilient school bears the mark of a woman who resisted with all she had: her patience, her tears, and her humble bread.

In this book, we open the pages of these stories to write about women who did not seek heroism but were made symbols of resilience by life itself. These are Women in the Hell of War, and in each one lies an unforgettable tale of resistance.

The Gaza Strip

The Gaza Strip is divided into several major cities and Palestinian refugee camps, each with its own unique character that reflects a long history and rich social and cultural diversity.

Gaza City

Gaza City is the beating heart of the strip, serving as its administrative and cultural capital. Located along the coast, it enjoys a strategic position on the Mediterranean Sea, making it a vital commercial hub throughout history. The city is a meeting point of traditions and heritage, where ancient markets like Al-Zaytoun (Olive Market) and the Gold Market coexist with modern life. With a population of around 600,000, its neighborhoods blend historical charm with contemporary urban expansion.

KhanYounis

Located in the southern part of the Gaza Strip, KhanYounis is the second-largest city by population. Known for its agricultural significance, it boasts vast farms producing fresh vegetables and fruits that supply the city and other parts of the strip. Historically, KhanYounis carries traces of centuries of human settlement and holds a prominent place in the national resistance movement. Its residents embody traditional Palestinian values, preserving customs and social cohesion.

Rafah

Rafah lies at the southernmost tip of the Gaza Strip and is renowned for the Rafah Border Crossing with Egypt, a lifeline for residents during times of siege and partial blockades. Despite political upheavals and challenges, Rafah remains resilient, with a diverse population engaged in agriculture, trade, and vibrant social and cultural activities.

Beit Lahiya and Beit Hanoun

In the northern part of the strip, Beit Lahiya and Beit Hanoun stand out for their relative calm compared to other areas, though they also face economic and social hardships. Beit Lahiya is celebrated for its beautiful agricultural landscapes, while its people take pride in their folk traditions and strong community bonds. Beit Hanoun, despite its small size, has a large population and plays an essential role in local trade and craftsmanship.

Palestinian Refugee Camps

Alongside the main cities, Gaza hosts several refugee camps, such as Shati (Beach), Nuseirat, Maghazi, Deir al-Balah, and Bureij. Established after the Nakba of 1948, these camps house more than half of the strip's population. Though living conditions are harsh, they remain symbols of Palestinian resilience and hope for the future. These camps preserve a culture of resistance and unwavering determination despite loss and displacement.

Life in Gaza Before the Wars

Before the recurring wars and blockade, life in the Gaza Strip thrived with vibrancy. Markets were bustling with local and imported goods, cafes were filled with friends and families, and children played in the streets and parks. The geographical diversity – coastal areas, fertile farmlands, and residential camps – created a rich social fabric united by shared struggles and aspirations.

Residents exchanged traditions, celebrated national and religious occasions, and worked tirelessly to build a stable future for their children despite challenges. From large cities to small camps, Gaza felt like one big home, inhabited by a united people under the banner of Palestinian identity.

The Impact of War and Siege

With successive wars, the landscape of life in Gaza changed drastically. Widespread destruction targeted infrastructure, homes, schools, and hospitals. The ongoing blockade led to a severe economic crisis and escalating humanitarian suffering, resulting in acute shortages of basic necessities like food, medicine, and electricity.

Internal displacement became a daily reality for tens of thousands of residents who fled their homes seeking safer areas within the strip. Normal daily life gave way to fear and uncertainty, disrupting work, education, and healthcare services. Psychologically and socially, the impact was profound

iii

– markets no longer buzzed, cafes emptied, and laughter disappeared from the streets. Scenes of sorrow, destruction, and bloodshed replaced the once-lively atmosphere, reflecting the depth of suffering endured by the people of Gaza.

Through it all, however, the spirit of resilience persists, a testament to the enduring hope for peace and a better future.

Preface

Women of Gaza... Unbreakable Resilience

In the heart of this endless cycle of pain and destruction, where the scene shifts between war and ceasefire, the image of the Palestinian woman in Gaza emerges as a living symbol of unbreakable strength and undying will. The women of Gaza, who have been and continue to be the backbone of life, bear responsibilities on their shoulders that surpass the limits of human endurance amidst extraordinary circumstances of siege and aggression.

The woman in Gaza is not merely an individual surviving in a harsh environment; she is the greatest beacon of hope in a society plagued by displacement and ruin. She is the mother who loses her children yet continues to sow life and compassion in homes that have collapsed and walls that have crumbled. She is the sister who stands by her siblings despite her wounds, the wife who maintains the resilience of a home shrouded in darkness, and the daughter who dreams of a future different from the painful present.

The women of Gaza live on a dual battlefield: the battle for survival in a besieged and shattered environment, and another against societal norms that impose restrictive roles on their freedom and movement. Despite these challenges, they have redefined everyday heroism, becoming leaders within their communities and sources of inspiration for those around them.

Their acts of bravery extend beyond confronting bombings and destruction. They resist poverty, challenge social constraints, and persist in pursuing education, work, and giving back. In every home in Gaza, the stories of women echo tales of patience and determination – from preparing meals over firewood to teaching their children by candlelight, from organizing psychological support for displaced families to participating in medical relief efforts.

These women are beacons of light in the darkness of the blockade, illuminating the path for future generations and proving that the Palestinian spirit cannot be broken. Their stories are not mere tragedies or tales of displacement but living testimonies to the strength of the human spirit that insists on survival, creativity amid destruction, and rebuilding amidst the rubble.

In the pages of this book, we paint a realistic picture of their world. We delve into the details of their daily lives, in moments of both vulnerability and strength, in their dreams and their pain, to carry their voices to the entire world.

You will read stories of mothers who lost their homes and loved ones, of homemakers who proved that life goes on despite loss, and of students and creatives who refuse to let their dreams be shackled by circumstances.

The women of Gaza are the invisible force from which the city draws its spirit. They are the fabric that sustains the continuity of life. Through this book, we honor this resilience, celebrate these silent acts of heroism, and bear witness to the fact that, despite everything, life persists there... and so do the women.

In The Name Of Allah:

But if you are patient and fear Allāh—indeed, that is of the matters worthy of resolve...

~Āl-'Imrān: 186

Contents

I am from Gaza…

I am from there… from the rubble,
From the debris smoldering in the dark.
I am from Gaza, from a land that births a thousand martyrs each morning,
in silence, in peace.
I am the cry, the voice, and the echo in a wound that walks without dignity.
I have lived displacement, my child has starved, and my dream has been
lost.

I have a mother who weeps, seeing nothing but smoke staining the walls.
I have a brother beneath the rubble, calling out… but no one answers,
except the sound of breaking spirits.

In my heart, I carry my city…
A city crumbling under the shelling,
And a little girl who once drew life,
But died before she could sleep.

I am from there… don't ask me…
How I live without a face, without identity.
I am from Gaza, from a homeland born in pain… and lost in the chaos.

~Ahmed Nezar Zeyad Helles

The Narratives

Shaima

The Night of November 10, 2023

We were displaced, staying in my sister's apartment, which was supposed to be safer (near the Meat Market) than our home in the Shuja'iyya neighborhood. But fate had other plans. It was 1:00 AM when I heard the sound of a plane so close to the window of the room where I was sleeping with my older sister, my mother, my younger brother, and my brother's children. The noise was terrifying, explosions echoed all around us, and we knew danger was near.

Without hesitation, we prepared to head down to the building's basement for shelter. But before any of us could even finish putting on our abayas or hijabs, a tank shell struck the apartment directly. My father was martyred instantly, his pure body torn into two halves, separated from each other. My beloved sister was hit by shrapnel all over her body, unable to move or save herself. She screamed in agony, "My children, oh Allah, spare my children!" My older sister was also injured and lay on the ground, calling out for her kids, "Maria! Aboud"!

As for me, when the shell hit the apartment, rubble began falling on my head, and dust filled my mouth, choking me. I felt myself slipping, about to collapse onto the hot stones beneath me. But by Allah's grace, I was saved. The apartment was pitch dark, but the force of the explosion blew open the door, allowing a faint light to filter in. I ran toward the door and found my younger brother and my sister's children standing there. My brother had bruises and cuts on his head, but thank Allah, the children were unharmed.

The four of us rushed to the building's basement, seeking refuge until the shelling stopped and we could go back upstairs to rescue the others. But the bombardment and direct gunfire on the building continued for hours. As we descended the stairs toward the basement, I cried hysterically, screaming to my brother, "I can't hear anyone! Not a single one of them is responding!" We were trapped in the basement, and every time one of us moved toward the door, bullets were fired directly at it. I was terrified that the building might collapse on top of us. I prayed desperately to Allah, hoping that my mother, older sister, younger sister, father, and everyone else were still alive so we could help them.

At that moment, I didn't yet know that my father had already passed away, the shell had split him in two. In my fear, I hadn't noticed that my wrist was bleeding profusely, nor that I had burns on the soles of my feet. After some time, the pain started to set in. My eyes never left the children, scared of what might happen to them. They kept asking me, "Where's Mommy?" And I would answer, "Mommy's upstairs, busy, but she'll come down as soon as she's done." My heart ached, and I couldn't stop crying.

After an hour in the basement, my younger sister stumbled in, her face and clothes drenched in blood. She collapsed onto the bed in the basement, unable to stand. She had been shot by a quadcopter drone, a bullet lodged in her abdomen and shrapnel in her back. She was on the verge of death; her body grew cold, and she nearly passed out. But I held her hand tightly and began reciting verses from the Quran. Slowly, she regained some strength.

Time seemed endless, and our hearts raced with fear. We had no idea what fate awaited us or what had become of our family, were they alive or dead? My brother Ahmed couldn't bear the wait any longer. He went upstairs to check on our mother, father, and sisters. It was then that he realized our father had been martyred. He saw our mother lying on the ground, bleeding. He tried to pull her to safety, but she screamed in pain, her back was likely broken, and the floor was covered in sharp debris and stones. He stopped dragging her and attempted to lift her despite her weight. But the despicable criminal entity wouldn't let us try to save those who might still live. They opened fire directly on my brother, forcing him to retreat and hide behind the wall.

Like any mother who thinks of her children before herself, my mother asked Ahmed, "How are your sisters, and where are they?" He reassured her, "The girls are fine, they're downstairs in the basement." At that moment, she smiled weakly, comforted that we were safe. Ahmed returned to the basement after giving up hope of rescuing our father. He found my sister Hiba and our father as martyrs but hid this from us, fearing the shock. Instead, he told us they were all alive but injured.

Time dragged on painfully. Suddenly, my older sister Nisreen and her son Omar arrived to rescue us after Hiba had called them before her martyrdom, telling them that we were all gone (as she believed). Then my eldest brother Mohammad came to assess who was injured and take them to the nearest hospital. We left with a group of people raising white flags, signaling to the criminal entity that we were peaceful civilians. We walked barefoot and wounded from the Meat Market area to the Industrial Zone, where my brother's house was located. When we arrived, we all broke down in tears, waiting for Mohammad to bring us news. When he finally came, he delivered the worst news of our lives: "Dad has passed away, may Allah have mercy on him."

We could only say, "We belong to Allah, and to Him we shall return." That same day, we were forced to flee the Industrial Zone for the Zaytoun neighborhood, where my brother Hossam's house was located, as the situation in the Industrial Zone had become too dangerous, with shells and missiles everywhere.

We couldn't reach a clinic or hospital, but the next day, my brothers brought a doctor to the house. He treated our wounds, removed the bullet from my sister's abdomen, and it took us months to recover physically. But the wound in our hearts will never heal. We were devastated that we couldn't bury the martyrs for two weeks after their deaths because the Zionists imposed a curfew on the area, targeting anyone who approached. It wasn't until the ceasefire was announced that my brothers went to bury them. What consoled us in our grief was the scent of musk emanating from my father's pure body, a dignity granted only to the righteous servants of Allah.

Days and months have passed, but their memory remains etched in our hearts and minds. May Allah have mercy on them, grant them the highest levels of Paradise, and grant us patience and solace...

Date Written: May 22, 2025

Dr. Alaa Al-Najjar

At Nasser Hospital in KhanYounis, Dr. Alaa Al-Najjar carried out her humanitarian duty as a pediatrician. Despite the thunderous sounds of shelling in the distance and the cries of wounded children echoing through the halls, she donned her veil and worked tirelessly to offer hope and healing to those around her.

It was just another day, or so she thought. Beneath the weight of her responsibilities, the anxiety of a mother lingered in her heart. She had left her ten children at home, safe and sound, or so she believed, far from the bombings and destruction.

But fate had other plans.

As she moved between the patients' beds, the devastating news pierced her soul like a bullet: "Your children... they've arrived at the hospital... martyrs."

She couldn't believe the words. The echo of that sentence was harsher than any explosion or cry for help.

One by one, they arrived, wrapped in white shrouds, their bodies bearing no signs of life, only the unforgettable marks of burns and charred flesh. Nine children, whom she had loved, raised, and named with such care, each name carrying meanings of hope and life.

Yahya, Rakan, Raslan, Jibrin, Eve, Reefan, Sayyid... nine souls gone in an instant, leaving an unfillable void in their mother's heart.

Her tenth child, Adam, was the sole survivor, lying in the intensive care unit, his small body fighting for life. Beside him lay her husband, critically injured, battling death.

Tears were forbidden, screams silenced. Though Dr. Alaa was a physician, she was now a mother who had lost everything.

She refused to leave her room, rejecting the cameras that tried to sneak behind her veil to document her pain. She refused to speak to anyone. Her only conversation was with Allah, pleading for patience and strength, asking Him to steady her heart as He had steadied the heart of Moses' mother.

On that day, Alaa was not just a doctor; she became a symbol of resilience, a story of a woman who bore pain beyond description, shouldering burdens that mountains could not bear.

The house she had left in safety was now rubble, the life she had dreamed of for her children turned to ashes in the fires of war. Yet, she did not lose her faith, nor did she surrender her dignity.

This doctor, who had taught her children the Quran and prayed to Allah to protect them, is now the story of an entire nation, a story of pain and endurance.

We pray that Allah replaces her sorrow with joy, strengthens her heart, lifts the anguish that has befallen her, heals her husband and son Adam, and comforts every Palestinian mother who has lost her loved ones.

Documented Community testimonies on social media

Date Written: May 28, 2025

Ebtihal Raheem

Age: 20 years

At dawn, the silence exploded.

It was an ordinary morning... or so we thought.

I woke up to the sound of my mother helping my little sister get dressed in her school uniform. I was still in bed, enjoying my day off from university, planning a simple outing that would bring joy to my heart and break the monotony of daily life.

My sister said excitedly, "Mom, I want to go to school early"!

Before my mom could respond, the sky suddenly lit up, not with the glow of dawn or the warmth of a summer sun, but with rockets piercing the calm of the morning, filling the sky with sparks of death.

And in that moment, the war began.

From the very first day, the news started broadcasting the names of the martyrs... and the numbers kept rising every hour. We stayed in the house, waiting, watching, and praying. In the first week, there was still a glimmer of hope in our hearts, a small hope that the war would end quickly, that we would return to our lives, and that this nightmare would be temporary.

But instead of things calming down, people began hoarding food, water, and flour. Shops closed, bakeries stopped working, and electricity was cut off. In an instant, we lost everything: light, communication, and even our sense of time... and slowly, hope began to erode in silence.

We stayed in the house for about forty days. Those were heavy days, filled with fear and anxiety. The sound of shelling never stopped, and the lighting was dim, or rather almost nonexistent, except for the flashes of explosions. We tried to live, eating very little, sleeping very little, our hearts hanging onto fear.

After forty days of the siege, someone's phone rang in the neighborhood. A young man answered the call, and we all heard the voice on the other end: "Evacuate the house... everyone must leave." It didn't specify which house; the entire street had to evacuate.

Suddenly, the street was in a state of panic. People were running, gathering their belongings, carrying their children, and everyone was searching for their families. I was holding my siblings, and Mom was with us, and we left the house. I was with my extended family, there were fifteen of us: my older

7

brother, his wife, and their young son were with us, and my older sister Haya, her husband, and their kids were with us too.

It felt like we were embarking on an escape into the unknown, not knowing if we would ever return or even if there would be a home to return to...

We headed to "Sitt Baba's" house, our grandmother on our father's side. She was 98 years old, yes, 98! And yet her heart was strong and her patience unshakable. She embraced us with her eyes before she embraced us with her home, and we spent the entire night there.

The next day, nothing happened... we returned to the house, but not everyone came back. Half the neighbors stayed away, too afraid to return, perhaps fearing ambushes or forced displacement. The street felt emptier, the voices of children quieter, and the movement of people slower... as if life was trying to return, but its legs were still trembling.

Less than a week passed after our return when we received new news: you must leave your homes; the situation is dangerous, and if you leave... there will be no return until after the war ends.

The words were heavy, as if they were stripping away the last bit of hope left in our hearts. We left again, and this time was harder because there was a feeling that this farewell might be final.

We went to my married sister's house and spent the night there, but oh, how difficult it was! The house was high up, and the tremors wouldn't stop. Every moment, we felt the ground shaking beneath us, as if the building was about to collapse on top of us. The sounds of artillery fire were beyond terrifying. None of us could sleep; we counted the seconds and watched the windows, while the news kept delivering shocks.

The next day, at the first light of dawn, we decided to leave the house. We left my sister's place, carrying what we could, and headed to the school, just as many others had done.

When we arrived, we found the school had turned into a shelter. My siblings had managed to bring some belongings from home and placed them in one of the classrooms. That simple classroom, four walls and a chalkboard, had become our temporary refuge, a place where we felt a fleeting sense of safety.

We stayed in the school for about a month, alongside our family, my uncle's family, and neighbors. We tried to adapt, counting the days as they passed. Every day, we packed our bags, fearing we'd be forced to leave. The news was terrifying: the war wasn't ending, and people were being told to flee because the army was advancing. Smoke bombs and artillery surrounded us, making the situation unbearable. My father decided it was time to leave, and we took whatever we could carry.

As we stood at the school gate, we cried because we were about to separate, especially since my married brother would be leaving with his in-laws. Halfway through the journey, we walked on foot with the children, then boarded a horse-drawn cart. All the while, we prayed to return, as rumors spread that men and young boys would be taken and killed, while women would be displaced.

When we reached "Al-Halaba," my father said, "We need to go back." Thank Allah, we returned to the classroom in the school. But we were in a hurry because they were firing rockets at anyone who lingered. When we got back, my uncle's family was relieved, because in such situations, safety means being with your loved ones.

Two days later, the situation worsened, and we were forced to flee again, to a school called "Al-Safad." When we arrived, we found our neighbors had already taken over one of the classrooms. They welcomed us warmly and made space for us. About 50 people crammed into the same classroom: my uncle's family, their children, our neighbors, and in the next room were my grandmother and her sister, my father's mother and aunt. As for the young men, they split into two groups: some stayed in the classroom, while others slept in the hallways on the floor.

The conditions were unimaginable: overcrowding, no privacy, and extremely limited resources. Every moment felt suffocating. But despite all this, being together gave us strength. In such circumstances, all a person needs is to be surrounded by their family.

On the second day in Al-Safad School, I saw my cousin (my uncle, who was martyred in the Farkhan War). He came to thank us, I had brought him three loaves of bread, and my mother had given them to him.

On the third day, he returned and said to my mom, "Eleven people ate from what you gave, may Allah bless your hands... Oh, how much we've suffered."

On the fourth day, news came that a ceasefire would begin at 7 a.m. I woke up with a small glimmer of hope. I took my younger sisters to the bathroom, and my 14-year-old sister hurriedly brought my nieces and nephews inside.

Suddenly, while we were still inside, the door burst open violently. My sister rushed in, terrified. Her fear was evident in her eyes, and outside, the sounds were unbearable, shells, bombs, screams, and bodies of martyrs in the schoolyard. Everyone was shouting.

I grabbed my sisters and my nieces and nephews, pulling them toward my mother. But my youngest sister, only four years old, froze in the middle of the courtyard, paralyzed by fear. She couldn't move. People were screaming everywhere! And I screamed at her, "Do you want to die? It's not our time yet!" I held her hand tightly, pulling and pushing her to move.

We ran back to the classroom, where chaos reigned. My sister fainted, and everyone was shouting at her to wake up. When I entered, I saw the classroom in disarray: shattered glass, people crouched on the floor with sheets over their heads, praying.

I went to my uncle and began praying with him:

"In the name of Allah, with whose name nothing can harm in the earth or in the heavens, and He is the All-Hearing, the All-Knowing."

And we didn't stop praying: "Oh Allah… Oh Allah"…

There was a small door leading to another school, and they started evacuating us through it. People were piled on top of each other, everyone desperate to escape death.

My uncle carried "Grandma" (my father's mother) in her wheelchair, but the chair wouldn't fit through the narrow door. Despite the danger, he lifted her and ran out through the main entrance of the school, his eyes focused only on protecting her. We escaped through the small door, me, my family, and my pregnant married sister.

As soon as we got out, we asked about my father and brother, crying because they weren't with us. We were deeply worried.

We saw some neighbors and asked about them. Thankfully, they reassured us that both my father and brother were safe, praise be to Allah.

As we walked along the road, I suddenly noticed my mother walking barefoot. She was lost in thought, her mind consumed with worry for her children, unaware of her own condition.

Amidst the crowd, someone had a pair of slippers in their bag. I quickly pulled them out and put them on her feet.

Afterward, we returned to the previous school, hoping to find some semblance of safety there. But when we reached the classroom, we discovered that our belongings had been stolen.

For a moment, there was silence, pain and regret filled the air. But we reminded ourselves: "Thank Allah, at least we're alive."

A week after the ceasefire, the war and tension returned, and so did the fear.

Six days later, my paternal cousin was martyred. Some youths from the neighborhood found him near the school, carried him, and brought him to the schoolyard. At that moment, the sound of tanks began approaching from the rear street.

They placed the martyr's body on a cart in the schoolyard, and every family retreated into their classrooms, fortifying themselves inside. We were trapped for two full days, unable to move or raise our voices, even our prayers were whispered while lying flat on the ground, as any movement could cost us our lives.

After the siege was lifted, we stayed in the school that had become our shelter. Though the word "adapt" felt meaningless, we tried to live day by day, carving out small moments of peace amidst the destruction.

We stayed there for about a month until that fateful day, the day they bombed the school bathrooms. The disaster was that our classroom was very close to them.

We heard the sound of shattering glass raining down on us, and people screamed in terror. The sound of fear was louder than anything else.

Without thinking, my immediate reaction was to protect my sisters. I grabbed a sheet, threw it over us as if to shield them from death, and we ran, to the section of my uncle's house. Inside half of the classroom, we hid behind the walls, our hearts trembling.

After a While, Things Calmed Down... But When We Came Out, We Saw That My Sister Ney had Collapsed, Her Hand Bleeding.

My heart sank with fear.

We ran to her, and thankfully, it was just a small wound, but it hurt. Yet, the pain of fear was far greater.

With a broken voice, I held her hand and said, "Thank Allah, this is our fate... Allah is our protector."

And everyone around us echoed, "Thank Allah, O Allah, protect us."

Despite the pain, we thanked Allah that she was still alive, as if survival itself was the greatest victory at that moment.

My brother, who is 20 years old, had only suffered a minor injury; thank Allah.

During that time, there were no supplies or enough essentials. Food was scarce, items were nearly nonexistent, prices were sky-high, and everything was extremely expensive. Aid trucks would arrive, and young men would rush to grab whatever they could. But fear was constant, everyone was running, everyone was pushing. Sometimes things turned violent.

Once, a young man's leg was broken near the trucks. Another time, someone was beaten with a stick. A third incident ended in death, and a fourth in theft...

My father refused to let my siblings go out, fearing he might lose them. He used to say, "Bread can be replaced, but a life cannot."

But sometimes, there was no other choice, you had to take risks for your family; you were forced to.

This situation continued until one day, our neighbor made some "Ghraibah" (a traditional cookie) and gave me a piece.

I loved the taste, it brought back memories of childhood, Eid, and safety.

And so, as an 18-year-old girl, an idea suddenly struck me:

"Why don't I start a small project? I'll sell Ghraibah! I'll help my family and support them."

I tried making my first tray, prepared by my own hands for my family, and they loved it. Their support and encouragement inspired me.

I suggested we make a larger batch and sell it.

And indeed, I gave my brother a plate, and he went to sell it to the young men in the schoolyard.

At that point, my father suggested that my sister's husband join us in the project, and that way, the whole family could work together.

Each of us worked in our own way, but we all supported one another.

We continued like this for about two weeks...

But unfortunately, happiness didn't last long.

One night, the shelling never stopped. Terrifying sounds of explosions filled the air, along with the cries of people mourning the martyrs, while our eyes were glued to the ceiling.

When morning came, we prepared ourselves because the sound of tanks was getting closer to the schools.

Sadly, we decided to leave the school.

My married brother and my uncle's family also left with us.

We didn't know where to go, the situation was incredibly difficult.

We headed to relatives of my uncle's family and stayed in another school called "Girls of Al-Zaytoun School."

There were no rooms, so they put us in the lab, the very lab that was supposed to be full of scientific tools had now become a shelter for people fleeing death.

We didn't have any belongings, not even a sheet. But thanks to their kindness, they gave us a sheet and a mattress, and my father bought two blankets.

We slept on the lab drawers, yes, the same drawers where we once sat preparing experiments had now become our beds.

All of us were close to each other, trying to endure the cold, fear, and anxiety.

We stayed there for four days, but on the fourth day... the attacks returned.

Shelling surrounded us, missiles, bombs, and there were casualties.

Early in the morning, my father had gone out but returned quickly, afraid for us.

By Allah's grace, a shrapnel hit the bike tire, not him.

The people were screaming, in the hallways, there was blood everywhere, and the place was unsafe.

We decided to leave, but it wasn't easy.

My married brother said, "Get ready... we must trust in Allah."

He was the first to step out of the schoolyard, and we followed him, walking through our fear, carrying patience in our hearts, and reciting in unison:

"In the name of Allah, in Whom nothing can harm"…

We recited Ayat Al-Kursi (the Throne Verse) and ran.

We headed to a farther area, to a place called "Hope Institute," a name that carried a strange contradiction, hope amidst a reality filled with nothing but pain.

We tried to find an empty classroom but couldn't.

My cousin came and told us there was an empty hall, occupied by only one family, with some space left.

We went there and settled as best we could.

My brother, may Allah bless him, didn't fall short.

He, my other brother, and my cousins worked hard, gathering some scraps and setting up a tent, not for anything luxurious, but to shield us from the cold, from prying eyes, and from despair.

We stayed there, counting the days anew.

There was no flour… life became suffocating. Despite the danger, my father went to the Al-Zaytoun area and returned with half a sack of flour.

But the flour was mixed with rubble, full of sand, and blackened.

Still, despite the difficulties… we ate and thanked Allah.

Because blessings aren't about their taste, they're about their existence.

And there were young men around us who needed bread. We gave them what little we had, feeling shy about how little it was, and they said:

"If only there were more people like you"…

That comment warmed our hearts, it reminded us that even in our suffering, something pure and human remained within us.

They bombed around the institute, and the corrugated metal above us started falling like stones on our heads. But Allah protected us.

A week passed, and my uncle, aunt, and grandmother, my mother's mother, arrived. My aunt had her orphaned daughter with her, about six years old. By Allah, there was a resilience in her that seemed far beyond her years.

They had been trapped in their home without food or water, but thank Allah, we were reassured they were safe.

We stayed in the institute for 15 days. On the 11th day, my father left early in the morning to go to the aid distribution point like everyone else.

From the start of the night, we were anxious... opening our eyes between every nap, whispering, "O Allah, please let him return."

I woke up in the morning to a whisper... My aunt and cousin were quietly waking up my brother, as if afraid someone might hear them.

I felt it... I sensed it from the atmosphere, from the voices, from the faces.

I asked them:

"What happened to Dad"?

No one answered... but my heart was pounding.

I went to my mom and said in a low voice:

"I feel something has happened to Dad"...

We went downstairs... My father's bicycle was still there, and his shirt was lying on it.

We asked the people around us, and everyone lied to us:

"He's fine, he's on his way back"...

But my mom picked up the shirt... She saw it, and it was covered in blood.

From her hand... her tears fell after the blood.

And all of us started shouting:

"Where's Dad? Is Dad okay? Answer us"!

We started crying and screaming.

Later, they told us the truth... My dad had been injured in his hand and was in the hospital.

The fear didn't leave us... but thank Allah, despite the severity of the injury, he was alive.

My father came back to us... Every day, they changed his bandages, and the medicine was expensive. We tried our best to afford it.

We watched over him, followed his progress, and prayed.

After some time, the army withdrew from Al-Zaytoun, and my uncle's family returned.

We stayed two more days to make sure Dad was okay because Al-Shifa Hospital was close to the institute.

Then we returned... We went to my sister's place, where she was staying elsewhere.

And by Allah's grace, she gave birth to a new baby.

By Allah's will, they named him after my father.

We felt life giving us something back, despite everything.

We reassured ourselves about them, stayed for a while, and then returned to the same school that had been our first shelter.

And we continued... for about three months, trying to live and keep our project going.

The "Ghraibah" cookies became a small symbol of our patience, our hold on life.

The whole family worked together... we gave it our health, pushed ourselves, sacrificed our time and days.

But the goal was one:

To protect our home, secure our daily bread, and remain resilient.

And thank Allah... the work succeeded, at least for a while.

Everyone tasted the sweetness of the Ghraibah cookies I made with my own hands.

And people started requesting them... for joy, and even for sorrow.

Even the sweet became meaningful in every moment, as if it softened the weight of the days.

Ramadan came... Ramadan is supposed to be the month of joy, gatherings, and peace... but this Ramadan was filled with fear.

And Eid came... and passed. A month later, we were displaced again.

But this time... it was a terrifying displacement.

In the middle of the night at 2 a.m., there was no light, no sound except for the whispers of people asking about their loved ones. Everyone was holding tightly to someone, afraid to lose them.

My married sister was with us. We were in a place close to her relatives, and we stayed there for a while…

But we tried to adapt, to hold on to each other.

We kept making "Ghraibah," and added new products to our efforts: chips and pastries, just so we could afford our necessities and feed our children…

We baked and counted the days, turning flour and hope into sustenance that kept us busy from the pain.

We were displaced twice after that…

Once to a school near my aunt's place, and once when we were trapped, trying to leave the area we were in, with snipers positioned on tall buildings.

We headed back to the school, which had been our first shelter.

We stayed there for a week, then returned to my sister's place, repeating the same scenario, but this time with heavier hearts.

The sound of shelling and the buildings collapsing around us was terrifying…

Suddenly, there was a wave of displacement from the Al-Zaytoun area…

My younger brothers were there, and they came to join us. Among them was my brother who was 21, soon to turn 22.

He stayed with us for a week… and what a beautiful week it was. By Allah, despite all the circumstances, he worked with us, slept beside us, laughed with us, and talked with us.

I saw in him the tenderness of a brother and a friend; whatever we asked for, he brought to us.

And he surprised me on the day I passed my Tawjihi exams, he gave me a mobile phone as a gift.

And one night… a night I'll never forget, it was strangely beautiful.

We all gathered, laughed, as if defying the sadness. That night, when we went to sleep, he was in the same room with me.

He hugged me and said, "I love you, and I want what's best for you."

17

He said the same to my sisters, as if bidding us farewell, but we didn't understand.

On August 25th, it was my birthday. I turned 19.

I made a cake, it wasn't perfect, but we ate it anyway. He said, "Thank you, it's delicious," and lifted my spirits.

I thought he was joking, but he ate it, even though I wasn't satisfied with how it tasted.

The next day, he helped Mom… and that night, I felt something was wrong. He couldn't sleep, and I was close to him… I picked up my phone, opened Surah Al-Kahf, and placed the phone next to him so he could listen.

He listened… and finally fell asleep.

He woke up early, prayed Fajr, and worked with us as usual.

And on this day, he went out to meet his friends… stayed away for two nights, and then returned.

He returned on a day we will never forget, September 1st, 9/1. His hair was shaved.

He came in to take a shower, asking where his clothes were hung to dry. Then, suddenly, he said with urgency: "I want to go and be martyred."

He heated water, washed himself… and when he came out, I joked with him, saying:

"If you're a groom, why did it take you so long to get ready in front of the mirror"?

"Come on, gather your strength, we need to get you married!" He laughed.

My mom had made rice pudding, and he said: "May Allah bless your hands, Mom, this is amazing"!

He took a plate and ate while standing by the living room door as we all sat together.

He gave us a look, a look I'll never forget, and called me over:

"Don't go out today… keep your face bright, shining."

But then he opened the door again and said:

"Mom, Dad gave me some money. May Allah protect him."

18

Even though my father hadn't given him any.

He closed the door behind him, only to reopen it moments later:

"Do you need anything? I'm leaving."

My mother told him: "May Allah ease your path and bless you."

He replied: "That's exactly what I wanted to hear… goodbye."

On that same day, at 3:30 p.m., "Allah granted him martyrdom."

I had dozed off for a bit when my married sister came running to me, calling me in a terrified voice:

"Wake up! They bombed Al-Safad School"!

My heart sank because my older brother was there.

And my brother, who was 22 years old, was martyred.

Everyone started running. When they arrived, the place was completely destroyed, and my brother was buried under the rubble. My older brother had been farther away from the scene. It was a massacre, the Al-Safad Massacre.

My beloved brother had become a martyr. He was just a few days away from turning 22, in October.

May Allah have mercy on him and grant him the highest levels of Paradise.

The news hit us like lightning, but deep down, we still held onto hope…

Hope that they would pull him out alive from under the rubble.

My mother, sister, and another brother went to the hospital to check if he had been taken there.

He wasn't there. But my sister called and said:

"Your brother is fine."

So we wouldn't break down in fear and tears.

I heard his voice… but, unfortunately, it wasn't his voice, it was my younger brother's, who is 16.

My sister told me:

"Go to Grandpa's house, and we'll meet you there."

They came... and everyone hugged each other tightly, crying and praying from the depths of our hearts that he would come out alive from under the rubble.

We prayed Asr (the afternoon prayer), and there was patience within us, a fragile hope clinging to our souls.

But... at 5:30 p.m., they pulled him out. He was a martyr.

We ran... we ran through the streets, trying to catch one last moment to say goodbye, trying to touch his forehead.

And we kept repeating his name, crying endlessly.

The young men carried him, running, and we chased after them to bid him farewell.

But when we saw him, he looked peaceful, as if he had truly ascended... a "groom," just as I had sensed in the morning.

Everyone gathered around him, crying, unable to believe it...

Everything we had lived through before felt like one world, and now we were in another.

My brother lay in the hospital courtyard. My father stood at his head, surrounded by everyone.

And I tried to hold myself together, to protect my younger siblings, my nieces and nephews, and my mother, who had collapsed in a way I'd never seen before.

Everyone was saying their goodbyes, and every farewell carried the weight of the sky.

I looked at my father, he stood by his head, broken, the first time I'd ever seen him like this: shattered, his voice gone, tears silently streaming down his face, the silent tears of a man weighed down by sorrow.

My youngest brother, sobbing, whispered to him:

"Forgive me... please forgive me. Why did you leave us"?

And my other brother, who is 20, couldn't bring himself to approach. He stood far away, collapsing from a distance, his eyes fixed on him as if his heart was screaming but no sound could escape.

My 14-year-old sister cried and called out:

"Where are you? Don't go! Please, come back! I'll do whatever you want"!

And my younger siblings, an 8-year-old girl and a 10-year-old boy, cried and screamed for their brother, the one who always made them laugh.

And my nieces and nephews, ages 4 and 5, and my older brother's son, who is 3, all of them gathered around their uncle's body, none of them able to believe it.

And my mother... she embraced him fiercely; she kissed him, leaned close to his ear, whispering prayers and reciting Quranic verses.

A mother who lost her son, can you imagine how she must have felt?

And I... I was the one who had endured everything until that moment. I had held on to hope, endured the pain... but that moment... it was stronger than me.

I broke down.

I'm the girl, 19 years old, who dreamed of celebrating with her brother, being his support, and having him as mine...

Suddenly, they said: "Let's go bury him."

I snapped awake, screaming:

"Please... wait! I haven't said goodbye yet! Please, let me say goodbye"!

I read prayers, looked at him, kissed him, and whispered into his ear, my heart aching:

"Please, answer me... they lied to us, you're supposed to come back! Please, wake up, open your eyes, tell me you're not gone"...

But he didn't open his eyes. There was only peace on his face. And I cried, saying to him:

"May Allah make it easy for you, He has chosen you... and how blessed you are, my martyr brother."

They buried him, and how difficult that word is... and we returned to the place we had been staying, but it no longer felt the same. Everything felt empty, cold.

Our nights were filled with tears and memories, no appetite for food, no desire to live.

We tried...

A month and a half after his martyrdom, I decided to start memorizing the Quran.

We tried to move forward, to keep going. We worked for a month, but then work stopped.

Life became expensive, and there were no schools to attend. We counted the days, waiting for the ceasefire.

And when they announced the ceasefire, we were supposed to be happy... but instead, we cried. We wanted our brother to be with us.

We decided to return home, but the scene was tragic. The house was destroyed.

But thank Allah, we cleaned part of it and settled in, grateful for even that small comfort.

We returned to try to live in a small space, and the day came when people began returning from the south.

Some of my uncles and aunts who had been in the south returned and immediately went to the hospital because my grandmother (my mother's mother) was there, and it seemed death was nearing her.

They saw her... and the next day, she passed away.

May Allah have mercy on her and grant my mother patience in her loss.

We settled for a while, but unfortunately... the war returned in Ramadan, the third month, and it was as if the pain had not been satisfied.

And then the Eid came... but it wasn't an Eid.

They even bombed the swings... they took away the children's joy.

And we... we kept trying, living... but life had become something else,

Our souls still carried the wounds; every moment we remembered the martyr, my brother...

And until today, the war continues...

Now it's May 2025, and we're still living under fire, under pain.

But in our hearts... there is light, there is hope that the war will end. Hope that aid will come, hope that life will return, even if just a little.

The situation is very difficult. There's no flour, no food supplies for months, and no aid is getting through. Gaza bleeds every day.

People rush to the distribution points, but not everyone gets anything.

And the scene? It's not normal, everyone is on top of each other, everyone just wants to live, to eat.

We have suffered greatly, breaking our fast with just two spoons of soup or a small piece of bread to sustain us.

We started mixing pasta with lentils, with a little flour... just to cook something.

We cook without flavor: no salt, no sauce, no spices... and that's only if we find something to cook in the first place.

But despite all this... we endure, we try, and we believe because our Allah is great... and He does not forget anyone.

The war will end, we'll laugh again, and Gaza will remain standing...

Despite the pain, despite the siege, despite the hunger.

And we don't know what will happen, will we survive? Will we be martyred? Will we disappear suddenly like those who have gone before?

Things don't stop... every moment counts.

But as long as we are here, we will continue to write the story,

We will keep talking about the martyrs, about the pain, about resilience, about Gaza...

Gaza... Gaza... it's not just a city,

Gaza is a story of patience, and we are its heroes, living on hope... and hope must remain.

Date of writing the story: 2025/05/17

Noor Al-Huda Abdul-Raheem Al-Arear

Age: 20 years

Allah says:

> *Those who have been evicted from their homes unjustly*
> *except for saying, "Our Lord is Allah"*

And so begins the story...

We weren't searching for heroism; we were simply trying to survive.

That night was different, heavy, suffocating with gunpowder instead of air.

The night in Gaza wasn't silent as it should have been.

It was pitch-black from the intensity of the shelling, and the stars were lost behind the smoke.

After holding out for forty days, refusing to leave the home we had built with love and prayer,

We found ourselves rushing out blindly, overwhelmed by the horrors of that night.

We waited anxiously for dawn to break,

Hoping to see a glimmer of hope that would compel us to keep going,

A painful story, but one we hoped would have an ending that satisfied us and eased our hearts... And we're still waiting.

The story dragged on.

My mother sat, kissing the walls of the house as if bidding farewell to a child.

And me? I filled a small bag with my photos, memories, my Quran, and the poetry notebook where I had written about "return."

I didn't realize that I would become the poem myself, writing my story with both hands.

We walked on foot because there were no cars...

Carrying what cannot be carried: a child on one shoulder, an elder on another's back, heart upon heart.

We wore whatever we could find, carrying what could never be forgotten.

The road was an extension of pain,

No distinction between a mother and a child, between a passerby and a martyr.

We split up along the way, my father went east with my siblings, and we went west with my mother...

It wasn't a farewell; it was a tearing apart.

Every time we looked back, the house grew farther away, and the sky drew closer.

Midway, a shell fell near us, My little sister screamed, but no matter how loud her cries, no one among the Arabs heard her.

The Messenger of Allah spoke the truth:

"You are many, but you are like the scum of the flood."

I held her hand, and we ran, ran toward the unknown, where no place would shelter us, and no destination was known.

We stayed without shelter...

And at night, far from our home, on the pavement, my mother prayed.

She spread her prayer mat on the ground soaked with the blood of martyrs, prostrated herself, wept, and repeated:

"O Allah... We have no one but You."

And then, unexpectedly, a stranger extended her hand to us and said:

"Come to my place; you shouldn't spend the night in the street."

Her house was small, but her heart was wider than Gaza.

She gave us a blanket, warm bread, and a smile that said:

"There are still people who support, and Allah is still with us."

I remembered a verse of poetry I used to recite:

"And the best of Allah's creations is a man through whom He fulfills the needs of others."

At that moment, I realized that dignity isn't found in houses, but in prostration.

And displacement isn't the end, it's the beginning of a new story where Allah is the refuge.

We didn't lose; we only experienced how Allah honors His servants in the harshest trials,

How He creates warmth from fire, a home from exile, and an answered prayer from scattered hopes.

I am the daughter of that night, the daughter of prostration, the daughter of the house that no longer exists…

But it became a homeland within my heart.

But that night didn't end with the prostration.

When the sun rose, the city looked as if it had become a stranger to itself.

Its streets were filled with dust, faces pale,

Children didn't cry, they just stared, as if they had aged twenty years in one night.

I searched for familiar eyes among strangers,

No familiar voice, no laughter from my siblings, not even the echo of our old footsteps.

The first days of displacement passed like ages,

Moving from one house to a shelter, from a mattress on the floor to the bare ground.

Yet, even in those moments, there were sparks of light:

A woman cooked us soup after hearing us talk about hunger,

A man gave my brother his shoes because he was barefoot,

And a little boy drew a house and wrote on it: "We will return."

In every place we settled, people told their stories:

One woman lost her mother on the road,

Another gave birth to her daughter in the street under bombardment,

And an elderly man sat on a rock, glorifying Allah after miraculously surviving.

An invisible bond formed between us, of pain and survival,

Of patience and prayer, of loss and certainty.

As the Palestinian poet Mahmoud Darwish said:

"And Gaza does not sell oranges, for its blood is canned."

One night, as my mother prepared to sleep, she whispered to me in a soft voice:

"The house may be destroyed, but we're still here. Dignity isn't tied to the key of your house;

Dignity is to never deny Him, to always praise Him, even with tears in your eyes."

Her words became a pillar of hope.

I felt that we hadn't been defeated; on the contrary, we were the ones who remained human amidst the ruins.

We, despite everything, dream of returning, of building a small homeland in our memories,

And carry the key to our home like a badge on the chest of longing.

The first night of displacement ended, but it wasn't the conclusion.

It was the beginning of a long story, in which Allah is always closer than we think,

In which hearts cry but do not break,

And in which, despite everything, we survive... simply because we believe Allah is with us.

And until this moment: the sound of bullets still drowns out laughter,

And the cities still breathe under the rubble, searching for a day when dreams won't be bombed.

The war hasn't ended... it continues to write its chapters on the bodies of those who have nothing left but broken hope...

And unfortunately, we are still waiting for the end.

Date of Writing the Story: 2025/05/22

Olfat Nasser Abu Shahla

I am Palestinian, from Gaza. We are now displaced in Yarmouk Stadium. At first, we were in our homes, but then we fled to the south. We crossed the checkpoint and saw the Jews in front of us, women, men, and children lying mutilated on the ground. It was forbidden even to look back if something fell from your hands.

We reached the south, exhausted, until someone finally gave us a little water to drink.

We moved on to Rafah, where we went to schools and camps, spending nights sleeping in the streets.

We sold everything we had, phones and belongings, to provide food and drink for our children.

Here, we endured hardships that we could not bear.

We moved from one place to another.

In Rafah, we stayed in schools. Six families lived together in one classroom. We remained there for five months near the border crossing, but then we were warned against staying longer, so we evacuated to Tel al-Sultan, east of Rafah.

There, we found ourselves in empty fields. When we arrived, people donated tents, and we settled into them, joining the camps.

After three months, evacuation orders were announced.

Transportation was extremely expensive, and by that time, it had become necessary to leave Rafah. We left, spending what little money we had left.

We went to KhanYounis, where we spent two months as displaced people, exhausting every penny we owned. When we arrived, there was no water or drinkable supplies; both salty and fresh water came to us with great difficulty.

Life in KhanYounis was incredibly hard. We eagerly awaited the arrival of "Takiet al-Neswaan" (the women's charitable kitchen), and the women would go before the men to get a little food.

Water arrived only after long intervals.

Men, women, and children, all went out in search of water. Everything was difficult, and when we managed to get something, we rejoiced greatly.

Whenever we heard rumors of a ceasefire, we felt immense joy, but no ceasefire has happened yet.

One day in KhanYounis, suddenly, we were warned: "The Jews have entered!" Everyone began running barefoot, without anything, not even their papers.

Children didn't know where their families were. Everyone was crying, screaming everywhere.

It became necessary for us to flee again.

Where would we find money? We hadn't settled anywhere for long, just short periods.

We didn't understand what was happening.

At that point, we started thinking. Everyone pooled whatever money they had left to rent a truck.

Six families, with all their belongings, climbed aboard.

That night, we headed to Al-Nuseirat.

We arrived at a field filled with olive trees, it was pitch dark.

We asked a man to let us stay with him for the night, fifty families full of children, women, and men, seeking shelter just for one night until morning.

He eventually gave us a place to settle, so we pitched our tents and stayed there.

Flour was unavailable.

We bought a single loaf of bread for seven shekels.

Vegetables were priced so high that we couldn't afford them.

We bought everything piece by piece.

We spent sleepless, hungry nights, unable to secure anything, tears streaming down our faces.

Then one day, we returned to Gaza.

At that time, we had no money left, but we were overjoyed because we were returning to our land. Walking on foot became necessary.

We walked with our small children who could barely walk, leaving our belongings behind in the south because we couldn't carry them anymore.

We spent hours upon hours until we finally arrived.

Our homes were destroyed, full of rubble and burnt.

We slept two nights in the streets until we came to this camp.

Many of my family members were martyred, my sister, her children, and my father lost his sight. Life became unbearably difficult.

Date of Writing the Story: 2025/05/20

Maisaa

Age: 36 years

My name is Maisaa, and I am 36 years old.

I am a person with special needs due to complications from childbirth that affected me deeply. Since I was young, I have walked with difficulty, and my weight increased because I couldn't move much.

On the first day of the war, my older married brothers were worried about me. They arranged a car for me and insisted that I be the first to leave the house because we lived in the eastern areas of Jabalia, close to the borders of the occupiers. If the Israeli forces advanced, I wouldn't be able to run or walk quickly, especially since I take chronic medication for respiratory issues and blood thinners, which could lead to complications.

I moved with my brother, his wife, and their children to my sister's house, where we stayed for a month and ten days. Those days were incredibly difficult, explosions and fire bombs everywhere, fear and terror at every turn.

Then we endured an extremely difficult night. Bullets and shrapnel struck the building next to us, and the civil defense teams barely managed to get us out. We moved to another place, to some relatives.

By then, famine had begun, and conditions worsened. One day during the war, the Israeli forces entered on the ground, and my brother refused to leave, so we remained trapped for two weeks, no food, no water, no clean drinking water. The children were starving, and we were terrified. The army bombarded the area with fire belts, forcing us to flee. Every time I took a step, I fell. My brother would drag me, but I couldn't walk. I didn't have a wheelchair, and even when I tried to sit on one, the soldiers forbade it.

The army ordered us to leave everything behind and head west to Gaza. It was a long night spent in the streets until the sun rose. I felt immense pain, I couldn't run, walk, or do anything.

My brother, his wife, and their children were always by my side, never neglecting me, but my disability became a barrier with every displacement and move. I suffered greatly, falling repeatedly. With the siege and closed crossings, my brother couldn't bring me the medication I needed to prevent blood thinning.

I felt like a burden on them. My mother, who had kidney failure, had passed away before the war. My father suffered a stroke when our five-story home collapsed. My eldest brother was martyred, and my second brother suffered a brain stroke, leaving him unable to speak or walk.

The lack of food, hunger, and skyrocketing prices made it impossible for us to buy anything in this devastated land. I fell ill with severe anemia and needed blood transfusions, but the hospital refused to treat me because the blood bank was empty, no one could donate as people were starving.

My brother began scouring the markets for dates, milk, or anything he could find, adding to his already heavy load. On top of that, he had to care for his young children…

All of this happened after the flour and bread crisis. We resorted to eating animal feed, birds, and tree leaves. By Allah, we were exhausted.

My sister-in-law would go out searching for wild herbs like mallow and chamomile, and birds, while bullets rained down around her…

After some time, aid began to trickle in, not enough, but it was something, and we were overjoyed during those moments.

Date of Writing the Story: 2025/05/16

Dana Abu Al-Khair

Age: 23 years

I am Dana Abu Al-Khair, 23 years old. I was an ambitious young woman who programmed hope before programming applications. In my fifth year of studying Software Engineering, I ranked first in my class, alongside my colleague and dear friend, "Aya Al-Muqayyid," who was second in the cohort. We were two passionate young women, participating in global competitions, researching, innovating, and dreaming of becoming teaching assistants at our university after graduation.

But on October 7th, everything changed. That moment flipped the equation from knowledge and ambition to displacement and destruction. Six days into the war, Aya was martyred. She had fled her home to stay at her fiancé's house, where a missile struck... Forty martyrs in one house, including Aya, the partner of my dreams and journey.

As for me, my long journey of displacement began. My family and I moved from place to place for 13 months, carrying only what little luggage we could manage and the heavy weight of memories.

After six months of displacement, I was supposed to complete my studies to fulfill my graduation requirements. Despite all the hardships, I registered for my courses, but I didn't have access to electricity. I continued my studies through my phone, using the internet in open streets under the scorching sun.

All of this took place in a tent, a tent of displacement that brought me together with books, a small screen, and big dreams that still resisted.

I took my exams and completed the defense of my graduation project. That project was a tribute to Aya's pure soul, the companion of my journey who left this world physically but remained in every line of my achievements.

After the ceasefire agreement, we returned from the south to the north on foot, an eight-hour journey of exhaustion, fear, and prayer. We carried our weary bodies and hearts that could no longer bear another loss.

The journey wasn't easy. We walked through rubble, under the sun, our eyes searching for shelter or a patch of shade.

We returned to the ruins of our home... there was no house left to live in, so we stayed at my grandfather's house. There, in an unforgettable human moment, we reunited with my sister, whom we hadn't seen in months, and embraced her little child, a child born during our displacement, far from us

33

and the details of his early life. The reunion was an intense embrace between life and death, absence and return.

But the war didn't give us much time. After 40 days, the shelling resumed, and within just 14 days, we were forced to flee again.

On the fourth day of Shawwal, while fasting, we packed our belongings and entrusted my grandfather's house to Allah's care. Hours later, the news reached us: "The house has been bombed."

And here we are now... living without hope, without life, waiting for relief.

We've returned once more to a tent... as if displacement is our destiny, and the homeland only accepts us beneath its fabric.

Date of Writing the Story: 2025/5/24

Duaa Yousef Al-Omrani

Age: 37 years

Original Town: Street 10

Place of Displacement: Al-Shatia Camp

Life is truly beautiful, life was truly beautiful. But in our homeland, we now say: life was beautiful.

We were in the best of conditions, safe and secure, dreaming of a bright and radiant future filled with hope and happiness.

We used to go to school, play with our friends, and compete in the "train race" of learning and education. We would return home in safety and joy, eagerly awaiting my husband when he came back from work, bringing us all kinds of food and fruits that our hearts desired.

On Fridays, our day off, the beautiful and bright day, we would go to Gaza's sea, the beautiful sea, and live the most wonderful moments of our lives.

We cooked, went out, and ate delicious food. Truly, those were amazing and joyful days. We miss them, the food, the fruits, the laughter, everything.

We long for our old lives, for safety, for life itself.

I tell you this while shedding tears of sorrow...

Our neighborhood was bombed; nothing remains of it. Not a single street or place was spared, it was completely destroyed. I lost my friends, my neighbors, even my furniture and my beautiful belongings.

We miss watching our favorite movies on TV. I've been deprived of everything.

Every day, I wake up to the sound of shelling and gunfire. Martyrs, deaths, injuries, destruction, and death everywhere. Every day is displacement, every day is suffering, and every day feels unbearable for us.

We now suffer from a lack of food, malnutrition, fatigue, and the daily hardships we endure.

Yes, our lives have become hell, a nightmare.

Every day, we dream that this nightmare will end. Every minute, we hope it will be the last minute of the war.

Do we feel pain and torment when a missile strikes us? Do we feel anything if we die, or if planes bomb us?

This has become our dream, this has become our reality.

We think about how we might die and how we will survive tomorrow.

Finally, I say to you: To everyone who feels for us, to everyone who stands with us, to everyone who supports us, to everyone who helps us, to everyone who amplifies our voices, to everyone who follows our news, thank you all.

Truly, I have nothing but gratitude for you.

Stay with us, stand by our side, and carry our voice.

Do not grow weary if the war drags on longer.

Do not tire of following our story, my heart is with you.

This is my message to you. Today, as I breathe, I do not know if this might be my last message because we are living day by day.

Date of Writing the Story: 2025/4/6

Nidaa Maged Al-Manasra

Age: 37 years

Original Place: Gaza

Place of Displacement: Deir Al-Balah

The Story of My Family and the Bitterness of Displacement in the Genocide War

On October 7th, a Saturday at 6:00 AM, we woke up to the sound of huge explosions shaking the area. Missiles were flying over our heads.

We lived near the border area east of the city. In a state of panic and terror, we gathered some belongings and left without knowing what was happening or where we were going. We took only a few things and forgot important documents like identification papers.

We fled to another house seeking safety, but in Gaza, there is no safe place. The house we stayed in was very small and crowded, but we tried to live while running away from airstrikes and missiles.

Then, the occupation forces began intense shelling on several areas, whether by air or artillery. After a short time, we understood what was happening: many Israeli soldiers had been taken captive by the Palestinian resistance after breaching the borders and carrying out numerous kidnappings.

When we realized it would be a fierce war, the shelling intensified on the area where we were staying. So, we decided to flee again, this time to another house in a different neighborhood.

We received news that our home, where we had spent our happiest days and created countless memories, had been bombed. Our house, dreams, ambitions, and everything beautiful associated with it were gone.

After spending two nights in the new house, the shelling never stopped. We lived in constant fear and horror. The bombing intensified in Al-Zaytoun neighborhood, and the house we were staying in was hit. Fire, rocks, and shrapnel entered the house.

My sister-in-law was with us, holding her newborn daughter who had arrived after three years of waiting through a cesarean delivery. Stones and shrapnel fell on the baby, nearly suffocating her. If not for her father's intervention, she wouldn't have survived.

Our elderly grandmother, who used a wheelchair, struggled greatly to move from one place to another. Miraculously, we escaped. We emerged from under the rubble, unsure of where to go or what to do next.

We decided to head to Al-Shifa Medical Complex, hoping to find safety, believing that the hospital was the safest place in Gaza. Along with ten other families, we all squeezed into a narrow hallway. Nine of us sat on a single mattress. This space served as our sleeping area, dining room, and living quarters, and it also became a corridor for transporting martyrs, wounded, and injured people.

We slept sitting up, and the infant had no crib, no milk, and none of her basic needs met. We suffered from a lack of food and water and found it difficult to use the restroom. The smell of martyrs, blood, gunpowder, and wounds filled the air.

After enduring all this suffering, threats came against Al-Shifa Hospital, and a nearby building was bombed. Smoke, shrapnel, and debris filled the space where we were sitting. So, we decided to leave and head south, following the instructions in leaflets dropped on us by the Israeli army.

The hospital was surrounded by snipers, tanks, shells, and phosphorus bombs that choked us. By a miracle, we escaped just as the same building we were in was bombed.

We walked along Salah Al-Din Street, the so-called "safe passage", from Gaza City to South Wadi. Exhaustion and fear consumed us as we walked, leaving behind our dreams, memories, future, and beloved Gaza, where we grew up.

We reached the cursed checkpoint, filled with soldiers, tanks, and armored vehicles. They sat atop their tanks behind sand barriers, laughing at us mockingly.

We walked an incredibly long distance until our bodies could no longer endure it. We finally reached Khan Younis on foot, forced to spend the night outdoors in the courtyard of a school. Above us was only the sky, below us were Israeli drones, and the darkness enveloped us.

We hadn't eaten anything, nor did we have water. Later, we went to Rafah, where we found shelter in a classroom with five other families. We struggled to obtain food and water, lacked beds and clothes, and had none of life's basic necessities.

After a long period, conditions improved slightly in the school, and things gradually became available. However, the feeling of oppression, humiliation, and fear never ended.

The bitterness of displacement, the ache of longing for our homeland and its streets, persisted. We moved from one place to another, searching for safety.

Finally, a ceasefire was reached, and an agreement allowed us to return to Gaza. The feeling was indescribable, a mix of overwhelming joy and disbelief because we had lost hope of ever returning.

We began gathering our belongings and preparing to return to our homes, even if they were destroyed. More than a year and a half later, we returned on foot.

Seeing Gaza for the first time after displacement shocked us. Destruction dominated the landscape, and sadness filled everyone's hearts. We reached my grandmother's house, stayed there, and started cleaning the rubble and debris. After two weeks, we settled in, feeling a sense of security and eternal comfort after a long period of instability.

One dawn, however, we woke to the sound of violent shelling shaking the city. My dear uncle, his wife, and their two sons were martyred. We didn't know what to say or do.

The nightmare returned, bringing back the worst memories. We continue to search for safety and stability, moving from one place to another.

Date of Writing the Story: 2025/4/6

Dr. Maisaa Youssef Helles

Age: 35 years

Original Place: Al-Shuja'iya

Profession: Principal of Nufoz Al-Khair Educational School

We were living the best moments of our lives, busy with work and education, when suddenly everything changed. On the fateful day of October 7th, destruction, killing, and chaos erupted. I lost my dearest relatives, and the occupation destroyed my home along with all its cherished memories.

I fled to my parents' house near Kurfur Mall and stayed there for 14 days. Then, the occupation threatened the area, forcing us to flee again, to Rafah, specifically to Abu Hossam Shaheen's house, starting a new life with the Shaheen family.

I won't hide it from you; it was a happy life. They embraced me as if I were their daughter. Together, we prepared meals and shared conversations. Despite the pain of loss, we lived relatively happily. Every day, I thanked Allah for finding a home where I felt safe and not alienated.

On November 20, 2023, at 4:00 AM, I woke up in Al-Najjar Hospital after being injured when the occupying forces bombed the neighboring house of Abu Hossam Shaheen. Shrapnel struck my head, causing severe swelling on my face and eyes. For an entire month, I couldn't leave the house or see anything. Thanks to Allah, I fully recovered after a month of treatment. Those days were difficult; without His care, I might have lost my sight or one of my children.

Then came the ominous day when leaflets were dropped on Al-Jannina neighborhood. Here came the second shock: Where would we go? That day, I wished for death...

Later, I decided to seek refuge at Dr. Ashraf Qassas's house. He welcomed me, my husband, and my children warmly. Once again, I felt relief knowing I had a home rather than a tent. But happiness didn't last long. Leaflets were dropped again, this time on Tell Zaroub. The tragedy began anew: Where should we go???

Eventually, I decided to flee to Al-Nuseirat Camp, joining others from Gaza living in tents. Honestly, I was devastated at first. Memories flooded back: how I once lived in a luxurious house with elegant furniture, a car, and a chalet for my family in Al-Sudaniya. Before October 7th, my dream was to achieve a prestigious position in society. Now, without fault, I live in a small tent lacking the most basic necessities.

Today, dreams have no place in our lives. Our sole wish is to return to our homes or any of our relatives' houses. Oh, the sorrow and heartache we endure...

From here, I rose to help myself and the displaced. I initiated a project titled "Together to Ease the Pain of the Displaced" to support them materially and morally since they lack the basics: shelter, food, and drink.

I distributed cash gifts to displaced families and children of martyrs. Then, I thought about helping children in the camp. Thus, I founded Nufoz Al-Khair Educational School, registering students and conducting interviews with teachers based on experience. We encouraged students with activities like drawing, distributing toys, sweets, biscuits, clothes, and organizing daily group breakfasts. By Allah's grace, enrollment reached 500 students, and additional educational tents were opened.

Even now, after relocating from Al-Shuja'iya to Al-Shifa area, I continue working amidst difficult conditions, managing Nufoz Al-Khair Center and charitable initiatives to alleviate people's suffering as much as possible.

I pray that Allah uses our efforts to benefit us and guide us toward serving students in Balata Camp, the largest displacement camp in the central region.

And the question remains: Will we return???

What frightens me most is that the Nakba of 1948 may repeat itself, preventing us from returning. Perhaps the only memory left for us in Gaza will be the key to return...

During these bitter days, I am about to publish my new book titled "Jerusalem and the Sociology of Refugees." I revised this edition significantly because I originally wrote it before October 7th, discussing the suffering of refugees based on historical accounts. Now, having lived this catastrophe, this Nakba, and experienced displacement firsthand, I understand the true depth of suffering. Living in tents, enduring war, and lacking security are far more painful than any information conveyed through books.

Life in tents, overcrowded classrooms, inadequate seating, insufficient supplies, and poor ventilation make learning extremely challenging. The reality of displacement surpasses any description found in history books.

Duaa Youssef Helles

Age: 34 years

Original Place: Al-Shuja'iya

Place of Displacement: Al-Misahal Area

From Gaza... I am not writing these words to be read in a news bulletin, but to tell our story, mine, my husband Jaafar's, and that of our children: Youssef, Muath, Mohammad, Basent, and Toleen.

I recount days that pass as heavy as the stones filling our streets, and nights where we don't know if we'll wake up to see them again.

Since our house collapsed, we no longer know what safety feels like. We move from one corner to another, searching for shelter, for a wall that hasn't fallen yet, for a blanket to protect us from the cold.

Every morning, I leave with my husband carrying nothing but my worries, and every evening I return carrying feelings of helplessness.

Basent, my little girl who hasn't yet turned eleven, is sick. Cancer is eating away at her body bit by bit, and every day I stand before her, powerless. There is no medicine, no referral for treatment, no open crossings, nothing.

I look into her eyes, and without speaking, she asks me:

"Mom, when will I get better"?

Jaafar, my husband, tries to stay strong for us. We boil water, crumble bread, and hug Basent and Toleen so they won't feel the cold. But sometimes, late at night when we think the children are asleep, he breaks down.

Youssef, my eldest son, tries to act like a man. He carries water, helps me search for medicine, for food.

Muath and Mohammad play by the tent door. I watch them and wonder: What kind of childhood is this that they're living?

And Toleen, she holds her sister Basent's hand and says:

"You'll get better, right, Basent"?

And Basent smiles despite her pain.

One day, after hours of searching for treatment for Basent, I returned empty-handed. I sat next to her, rested my head on her small hand, and whispered:

"Forgive me, my daughter. I can't bring you the medicine… but by Allah, I try every single day."

She smiled weakly and said:

"I'm not afraid… I just want to go play a little."

At that moment, I felt completely shattered.

All that was left in my heart was a muffled scream, a mother's cry wishing she could take her daughter's illness upon herself, or sleep alone in the open so her children could have a warm bed.

This is our story, one of thousands of stories in Gaza.

We don't ask for miracles; we only want to live, to treat our children, to see their faces smile… nothing more.

Date of Writing the Story: 2025/4/6

Nidaa Youssef Helles

Age: 34 years

Original Place: Al-Nazzaz Street

Place of Displacement: Al-Misahal Area

I am a Palestinian citizen, living in Gaza, a city that now knows pain as intimately as it knows its people, memorizing the names of martyrs as it does the names of its old streets.

I lived a simple life within the walls of a house my father built with his own hands in a small neighborhood where everyone knew each other. We didn't have much, but we had security in family moments, warmth in a plate of fava beans every morning, and smiles that emerged despite the hardships of life.

Then came a day, not like any other day. Explosions thundered, not once but repeatedly, and the walls of the house collapsed just as my spirit did. There was no longer a house, no longer a neighborhood.

We fled. We scattered. My children slept on the ground, and the sky rained fear and cold instead of rain.

We didn't have enough food, nor medicine to heal wounds or silence moans.

I saw death many times, but I truly understood loss when I held the body of my friend Batool, killed while searching for bread.

In every moment, I asked myself:

Why? Why must we live in fear and die in silence?

Why doesn't the world understand that we carry only our souls, and all we ask for is life?

Today, I live lost between a tent and a street, without an address, without a safe homeland. All I have left is my Nidaa Hilles.

I write it on the walls of the displacement camp, hoping someone will remember that I was once a human being living in Gaza.

Date of Writing the Story: 2025/4/20

Alaa Yousef Helles

Age: 44 years

Original Place: Northern Rimal

I don't know if my words will suffice to express the bitterness of what I've endured through displacement, fear, hunger, and oppression.

Like many mothers, I carry not only my burdens but also those of my husband and children on my shoulders. I feed them not just with food but with hope, hope in Allah, that after hardship comes relief, and after difficulty comes ease.

At times, we were closer to death than ever before. Every time the shelling intensified, I would rush to my children, hold them close to my chest, and reassure them that everything would be okay.

During my first displacement, from Gaza to KhanYounis, I was blessed by Allah to meet kind people who took me in and treated me well.

Months of displacement passed while I stayed with "Umm Rami," who became like a loving mother to me, treating me as one of her daughters.

Days passed with their joys and sorrows, and I vividly remember the days when famine began. They were difficult times, and I recall Umm Rami dividing a loaf of bread among us.

The hunger and exhaustion I felt were nothing compared to seeing my children starving. Their frail bodies broke my heart, and my helplessness killed me inside.

Whenever my head bowed under the weight of sorrow, I quickly found Umm Rami's shoulder to lean on. Our conversations and shared stories eased the loneliness in my heart. We cooked together, ate together, cleaned, and organized the house together.

The shelling intensified, and the killings increased in KhanYounis. The day we long feared arrived, the second displacement, and saying goodbye to Umm Rami.

It was a heavy day. I hugged her, thanking her with faint words choked by tears. She parted from us with hope in her heart that we'd meet again in better circumstances.

Our second displacement was to Rafah, and soon we were forced to flee repeatedly. Our final displacement was to Mawasi in KhanYounis, where we spent bitter days in a tent that offered no protection from the summer heat or winter cold.

Then came that day, the day I received the news of Umm Rami's martyrdom.

The news struck me like lightning, and my chest tightened with unbearable grief. All I could say was:

"To Allah we belong, and to Him we shall return."

I couldn't find better words of mourning than my tears falling in longing and sorrow.

I tried to console myself over losing Umm Rami, after the war tore me apart from my family and loved ones, leaving us displaced and scattered.

On the day her pure body was laid to rest, I repeated the poet's words:

"I never knew, before your burial in the earth,

That stars could sink into the soil."

I found no solace in words, except that Umm Rami had moved on to Allah's mercy and favor, and that we would meet her in paradise, Allah willing.

In conclusion, I want to say that our lives weren't entirely bleak. Often, Allah's kindness shone upon us, bringing light and relief even in the darkest of days. How could it be otherwise? Allah is gentle with His servants.

Date of Writing the Story: 2025/4/7

Jana Mohammad Rajeh

Age: 20 years

Original Place: Jabal Al-Rais

Place of Displacement: Tuffah Neighborhood

I lived in a simple house with my family in Al-Sha'af. On October 7th, I fled with my family to Abdul Fattah Hamouda School along with my eight siblings from my father's second wife. We faced countless hardships and miseries, extreme cold, hunger, thirst, and immense pain.

We often went without food because we didn't know how my father would provide for us, especially with the skyrocketing price of flour, which became unaffordable. We couldn't secure food, clothing, or water. We entered through the so-called "safe passage," amidst gunfire.

After enduring great suffering at Al-Salam School, we moved to Karam Abu Salem Crossing, where we stayed in a tent by the roadside for two full months. Then we were displaced to Mawasi in Rafah. With every displacement, we faced mounting difficulties and wished for death to escape this unbearable life.

We had no food, no water, no clothes, and not even blankets. We experienced immense suffering. My brother was critically injured when our home was targeted; may Allah heal him. My sister is battling cancer; may Allah heal her as well.

How much we suffered from hunger and the scarcity of flour! We endured immense pain, going to bed hungry and waking up to an empty stomach. Praise be to Allah in all circumstances, we live and die every day from the lack of food.

What did I and my siblings do to deserve this life? We long for food, bread, and the simplest things, yet we are deprived and left starving.

Rahma Naif Abu Qas

Original Place: Tuffah Neighborhood

I am a woman like any Palestinian woman. We lived in the Tuffah neighborhood of Gaza. I was married when a shell struck our wall, filling the room with black smoke. In the living room, I was holding my stepson's baby, and I ran out into the street with the child crying loudly, screaming for his father: "Come"!

The mother came out upon hearing her son's cries, took the baby from me, and said: "If it's written for him to be martyred in his mother's arms, then so be it." Not even a word of thanks was given to me.

We weren't on good terms. Later, we fled to the south, to Rafah, where I lived in a tent with my husband. Conflicts arose, and eventually, we divorced. That's when my suffering truly began.

I returned to my mother, feeling like a victim, while everyone blamed me. My father had passed away, and the news of his martyrdom reached me while I was still with my husband. The divorce caused disputes, and he refused to believe that I wasn't at fault.

In anger, my husband told me: "Leave." I left, and he never believed me. He listened to his daughter but not to me, he trusted them over me.

My mother, now a widow, had no one else to rely on. She was staying with my brother, whose wife had divorced him. We ended up on the street outside Telsultan Boys' School. When my husband divorced me, it was winter, and the weather was bitterly cold.

I climbed onto a donkey-drawn cart alone, crying, unsure of where to find my family. I told the driver about the school, and he said, "This is where my children study," and he took me there.

I was mentally scattered and in shock, lost in the unfamiliar southern region where we had no one. My mother fell ill, and I didn't know what to do for her. She stayed with my brothers in a tent, but they mistreated her, refusing to care for her properly, even begrudging her a single tomato.

One day, a kind woman visited the tent and showed compassion toward me. She brought chamomile tea, though I didn't have money to repay her kindness. People tried to help, but I was overwhelmed with grief and couldn't stop crying. I'd go to the charity kitchen to feed my mother, waiting two hours in line, only to find no food left when it was my turn. These struggles exhausted me emotionally and physically.

The news of my father's death hit me like lightning. Every time I see an elderly man, I think of my father. They robbed me of security. In Shuja'iyya, an elderly man was shot by a sniper. May Allah hold them accountable.

These were two devastating shocks, yet I couldn't afford to break down. Despite being emotionally and physically shattered, I had to persevere.

Living conditions were unbearable, the shared bathrooms were filthy and exhausting. Alone, I cried, while my paralyzed mother depended on me. Her sons shamed her and barely provided for her, forcing her to beg for twenty shekels just to survive.

The doctor administered IV fluids and sent her back to the tent. Carrying her throughout the journey drained me. I prayed to Allah for strength.

Later, I wandered to Al-Zawayda, lost and broken. For a week, we camped near the sea, and my mother grew sicker. We then moved to Deir al-Balah, staying in a classroom. Poverty and hunger plagued us. I struggled to endure, reduced to begging from strangers, overwhelmed by tears and despair.

Where could I go? Where could I belong? I scavenged fields, crying in frustration. It felt like a nightmare I couldn't wake up from. What catastrophe is this? No father, no brother, no husband, everyone abandoned me and my mother.

Eventually, we were placed in a tent in KhanYounis, surrounded by filth, insects, and biting cold. Both my mother and I wept endlessly. Food and water were scarce, and we relied on charity kitchens.

My mother, already sick and bedridden, suffered further indignities. Neighbors mocked me: "Where are you alone"?

My life has been filled with torment to this day. Returning to Gaza, I found my siblings looting our home and occupying it, along with my brother's wife. They treated us cruelly, mocking and betraying us.

They said to me: "We're not obligated to feed you. Go back to the south."

I witnessed unimaginable humiliation without money. The burden weighed heavily on me, known only to Allah.

A woman in the south showed more compassion than my own family, she became both a sister and a friend to me.

Truly, I felt like I was losing my mind, confused and unable to act. How could I care for my dying mother, who cried endlessly from hunger and despair? Vermin infested our tent, and I wept bitterly.

Never had I imagined such suffering.

Watching hunger and fear felt like watching a tragic movie. No one supported us, moving us from one tent to another.

"Take your mother and feed her," they'd say.

But where was humanity during the war?

Desperate, I called out to people, my voice weakened by exhaustion. I found no savior except Allah.

I nearly lost my sanity.

To this day, I have no father, no home, I am orphaned.

Why did this happen to me?

For my mother's sake, I endure. She has no one else.

Every second, I wish for death. By Allah, death would be kinder than this humiliation.

My older brother once hit me and asked: "Are you starving"?

Yes, we starved.

Instead of being my support, this brother turned against me.

I wandered the streets, unable to defend myself, while my mother's illness worsened because of me.

She has only Allah, and me.

Her other son, my stepbrother, doesn't deserve to be called my brother. None of them offered any support.

My husband was good and never neglected me, but misunderstandings drove us apart. After my father's passing, tensions escalated further.

He blocked my number, and later, he told me: "You've been divorced."

Divorce, a mere phrase, yet it shattered me.

He asked: "Where will you get maintenance? How will you eat"?

What could I do?

By Allah, life is unbearably hard.

Even today, I struggle to overcome what happened.

I wanted to return to Gaza, but my father remained on the wheelchair.

From KhanYounis, strangers took us but got lost along the way.

Good-hearted young men sympathized with me.

"Where are your people? Where are your siblings"?

I have no one.

They brought us to Gaza.

When I arrived, I broke down crying for my father, may Allah have mercy on him. Passing by our bombed-out house, I screamed uncontrollably. My father's room was destroyed.

Oh Allah, death and destruction everywhere.

Since the war began, our lives have been ruined.

Our physical and mental health has deteriorated.

I have no desire, no passion left.

I don't want to live.

I wish I had been martyred alongside my father.

All my relatives blamed me and distanced themselves from me.

I walked this painful path alone.

It's so hard, I can't get up, cry, sleep, and think about feeding my mother. I feel no safety.

No one brings comfort anymore.

The war made us fear everything.

But I must continue, for my mother's sake.

Allah willing, I'll persevere.

Everyone saw me caring for my mother, saying, "She loves her and takes care of her."

Allah chose me for this role.

And my ex-husband continues to haunt me, as I remain attached to him despite everything.

He was my entire family.

But after my father's death, we divorced within three days.

The psychologist warned me: "If you keep overthinking, you'll lose your mind."

The sounds of shells, missiles, and explosions echoed everywhere.

I screamed like a child.

By Allah, I'm exhausted, all alone.

I married late hoping for stability, for someone to take responsibility for my food and drink.

In the south, bread was scarce. There was no food.

I roamed between tents, begging for scraps.

Date of Writing the Story: 2025/05/15

Shaima Nezar Helles

Age: 20 years

Original Place: Northern Rimal

I have lived for 20 years, and during this time, I've experienced so much in this war. Let me tell you my story.

I had many dreams, one of which was to study engineering at university. But all those dreams faded into oblivion when this war began, a war that made everyone dream the same thing: for it to end.

At first, the war seemed like any other conflict that had come before. I never imagined what would happen next, what happened was unimaginable.

What happened to me was that I fled our home after the first week of the war, seeking refuge in KhanYounis, a place that wasn't as safe as people claimed.

Day after day, I waited to return to my home.

But this war didn't stop at one displacement, it forced us to flee multiple times. One of those displacements was to Rafah, where we left the house of Al-Sha'er family for the home of Al-Halawa family, who were truly the kindest part of this war.

When news broke about the invasion of Rafah, it hit us like a thunderbolt. KhanYounis felt like a graveyard, devoid of life.

In our third displacement, we found no shelter except tents, which became the worst days of my life during the war.

The tent couldn't protect us from the summer heat or the winter cold. I would wake up to drops of water falling on my face. In the summer, it was unbearably hot.

And the tent wasn't just uncomfortable because of its temperature; it was also too small to accommodate my family of nine.

Despite everything, I still dream of becoming an engineer, despite the tragedy, and Allah willing, I will achieve my dream.

Date of Writing the Story: 2025/04/09

Noor Diya Al-Natour

Age: 39 years

Original Place: Jabalia

Place of Displacement: The Camp

I used to live in a house near the railway tracks in Jabalia Camp. On October 7th, my family and I fled to the UNRWA clinic in the camp, where we stayed for two months.

My father was martyred in Beit Hanoun. Then, I returned with my mother to our house. We stayed in the camp for five months before fleeing again to the Al-Nafak area after the ceasefire.

I returned to my house, which had been completely destroyed by the occupation, and then we fled to a tent in the Al- Nafak area.

Here I am now, suffering alongside my siblings from hunger, a hunger only the grieving and displaced people of Gaza can understand.

All we ask for in this life is a loaf of bread, just enough to survive amidst the pain and oppression.

My mother is injured. May Allah have mercy on my father and grant him paradise, and may He give my mother the strength to raise us well.

Praise be to Allah in all circumstances. Allah is sufficient for us, and He is the best guardian.

Date of Writing the Story: 2025/04/30

Sahar Salem Qouta

Age: 47 years

Original Place: Tuffah Neighborhood

Before October 7th, I lived with my husband and children in our humble home filled with love, affection, and stability, the most important things in life.

We ate and drank from the bounties of the earth at affordable prices. But after that fateful day, we endured immense suffering.

I cannot describe the depth of our hardship. The word "suffering" falls short of capturing what we feel: the lack of security, the loss of loved ones, hunger, thirst, sleeping without safety, and a future shattered without achieving any of life's goals.

The land is stained with blood, and the cost of food and bread has become outrageously high.

We were displaced multiple times, and debts piled up due to displacement and rising prices.

Praise be to Allah in every situation.

Aida Mahmoud Rajeh

Age: 20 years

I used to live in a simple house with my in-laws. I fled to my parents' home, where we faced countless difficulties, conflicts, problems, pain, and poverty. I lost my dreams, suffered deeply, and our sole dream became securing a loaf of bread.

With skyrocketing prices, we resorted to eating wild herbs and weeds. Sometimes, we ground pasta or lentils to make bread, dividing it among the children just to ease their hunger. Other times, we stood in long lines at charity kitchens. Allah is sufficient for us, and He is the best protector.

Date of Writing the Story: 2025/05/05

Aisha Hashem Tamim

Age: 40 years

Original Place: Al-Attatra

Place of Displacement: Tuffah Neighborhood

I lived happily with my family in my home. On October 7th, missiles rained down from everywhere, and we fled to Hafsa School.

At the school, we faced numerous challenges. My husband is very ill and uses a wheelchair.

Later, we fled to Rafah, where I struggled with chest illness. There, we faced shortages of water and food, along with skyrocketing prices.

Then we fled to Al-Zawiyah area, and later returned to Gaza.

When the war resumed, we fled again to Al-Nafak area, living in a tent on the street, facing difficulty after difficulty.

Praise be to Allah in all circumstances.

The skyrocketing prices left us complaining of hunger and scarcity of food. When will our situation improve?

Praise be to Allah, despite the lack of medicine and rising costs. I humbly ask for your help, even in small ways, to meet our basic needs.

Date of Writing the Story: 2025/04/18

Sanaa Zaki Suboh

Age: 30 years

Original Place: Beit Lahiya

Place of Displacement: Al-Nafak Area

On the morning of October 7th, amidst the relentless roar of rockets, we were forced to flee to Hafsa School. It wasn't just a school for us, it was a temporary refuge in a sea of pain and suffering. There, within those cold walls, endless hardships and tragedies surrounded us.

I watched my little children cry without stopping, their eyes filled with fear and hunger, their small bodies trembling from the freezing cold. My husband, who suffers from heart disease, a herniated disc, and fluid in his lungs, was in immense pain but unable to do anything. He had no job, no medicine, and the lack of hope only deepened our suffering.

The burden I carried exceeded my strength, physical and emotional. I bore the weight of our entire family. Prices rose daily, food became an unattainable dream, and water was almost a luxury. Every night, my children and I cried together, clinging to one another in the darkness, searching for even a glimmer of hope.

Today, we live in a small tent by the roadside in Al-Nafak, facing hunger, pain, and fear. We have no shelter to protect us from the cold, no food to fill our stomachs, only hearts full of pain and patience. We dream of a day when safety will return to our children, and this darkness that has enveloped our lives will lift.

Date of Writing the Story: 2025/05/06

Samar Hikmat Abu Halima

Age: 45 years

Original Place: Beit Lahiya

Place of Displacement: Deir al-Balah

I lived in a beautiful house in Beit Lahiya. On October 7th, I fled my home as a newlywed bride, leaving everything behind. Later, we fled to Deir al-Balah, and after some time, we returned to our homes, but everything had been destroyed, even my new clothes and belongings.

We set up our tent on the rubble of our destroyed home. That tent became our refuge during this war. Then, we were forced to flee again with that same tent to Al-Daraj neighborhood, near the garbage dump, where we endured hunger, pain, difficulties, and countless tragedies.

Amidst the war, I gave birth to a baby girl. Alhamdulillah for everything, and Allah is sufficient for us, and He is the best protector.

Date of Writing the Story: 2025/04/19

Maria Youssef Diab

Age: 30 years

Displaced Since the Start of the War with Her Family

At the start of the war, we were forced to flee our home in the northern area and moved to relatives' houses in Jabalia Camp. We stayed there for about a week amid escalating shelling, destruction, fear, and panic.

Afterward, we fled to Hafsa School, but there was no empty space to sit, so we spent two full nights on the stairs, sleeping under the constant sound of shelling and fear.

On the morning of the third day, we decided to flee south to KhanYounis, where some relatives lived. We stayed with them for nearly a month amid a severe overcrowding of displaced people.

Then, we moved to a shelter for displaced persons at Sheikh Jameel School. Due to the extreme overcrowding inside the classrooms, we bought a small tent and set it up in the courtyard. We suffered greatly from a lack of money, winter clothes, food, and flour.

We experienced moments of sheer terror and fear, forcing us to flee again to Rafah without a tent, clothes, food, or even water.

During these difficult circumstances, my father separated from my mother, adding to our suffering. Since January, we have been living with my mother, with no responsibility from my father, not even a question about our well-being.

I took on all the responsibilities alone. My mother feared for us deeply and stayed up nights trying to secure our daily bread.

After the ceasefire, we returned north with my mother and stayed at my grandmother's house, where we remain to this day.

Date of Writing the Story: 2025/05/15

Esraa Salah Ajjour

Age: 25 years

On October 7th, the rockets and war began, meaning life stopped in all its details, work, play, freedom. Fear loomed over every place, and from that moment, I could no longer stay in my home.

I fled to my uncle's house and stayed there for three months. During that time, I was pregnant with my fourth daughter, "Rawiya," and endured all kinds of hardship. There was no water, so we filled buckets from the neighbors and carried them inside to use for drinking or cooking.

We cooked over open fires, and the foul smells spread throughout the place and entered my body, posing significant risks, especially since I was pregnant. I couldn't take any medications or vitamins, despite desperately needing them.

Date of Writing the Story: 2025/05/19

Sahar Salem Rajeh

Age: 47 years

Original Place: Jabal Al-Rais

Place of Displacement: Al-Shati'a (Beach Camp)

We were poor even before October 7th, and life was extremely difficult. I lived with my family of nine in a small house that barely fit us. When the war began on October 7th, we embarked on a journey of displacement and suffering. First, we fled to schools, then to Al-Nuseirat, and there we experienced every kind of torment, hunger, cold, fear, and deprivation.

But the cruelest thing we endured was the pain of hunger. Hunger spares no one, young or old. We went weeks without even a loaf of bread. We ate only lentils until we developed diarrhea from eating too much of them. Gaza was, and still is, under destruction, and we witnessed this devastation with our own eyes. We couldn't return to our homes due to the extreme danger, and my nephew was martyred while trying to go back to retrieve the remaining flour... he became "the Martyr of Flour."

Today, we live amidst suffering. No flour, no food, no safety. Our bodies nearly collapsed from hunger, and debts piled up with each displacement: transportation, tents, blankets... everything became exorbitantly expensive.

The skyrocketing prices made my family wake and sleep in hunger and fear, and I can no longer bear this pain. My heart aches every day, and my only wish is to see my family live in safety and find sustenance.

Oh Allah, ease our burdens and remove this affliction from us.

Date of Writing the Story: 2025/05/22

Hala Mahmoud Abu Halima

Age: 40 years

Place of Displacement: Al-Nafak Area

I lived in my house with my three children. On October 7th, I fled to Al-Shifa Hospital, then to Rafah. We endured every calamity of the war, witnessing the siege and destruction at Al-Shifa. We saw how the occupation forces entered, besieged patients, and left children screaming, hungry, and thirsty. The occupation destroyed our lives, homes, and hopes. Every day, we die a thousand deaths, wishing for death just to escape this unbearable life. Even bread, the simplest necessity in life, is unavailable; we don't eat it.

We eat weeds and wild herbs, longing for life, safety, and food. Allah is sufficient for us, and He is the best protector.

Date of Writing the Story: 2025/04/11

Rana Waleed Qouta

Age: 40 years

Original Place: Tuffah Neighborhood

I lived happily in my humble asbestos-roofed house in eastern Tuffah with my children and husband. Though poor, I felt secure and at peace. But on October 7th, when rockets rained down from all directions, we fled to Al-Daraj neighborhood.

We suffered greatly from the lack of flour and longed for bread. Every day, my children screamed and cried, wanting nothing more than a piece of bread, a pain that pierced my heart deeply. Oh, how we suffered from the scarcity of flour.

The problem didn't end there. Every so often, the crossings would close, the siege tightened, and we couldn't find bread. We couldn't afford it, how could we buy it when its price was exorbitant? We couldn't even purchase simple things to satisfy our children's hunger. How much I hurt for their pain, sorrow, and fear.

Date of Writing the Story: 2025/05/10

Islam Saleh Siyam

Age: 41 years

Original Place: Al-Nuseirat

Place of Displacement: Souq Al-Balat

We, the women of Gaza, witnessed the most horrific and vile massacres in history. This war surpassed all others in brutality, women, children, and elders were killed, and men were humiliated in cold blood.

And do you think our suffering was limited to death, destruction, fear, and loss? No, there is more… We lost stability and safety, moving from place to place with our tents just to survive. The greatest suffering was hunger, which spared no one. We, the children of Gaza, were deprived of the simplest rights to life, food and security.

Flour, an essential ingredient for life, was denied to us. To some, a loaf of bread may seem insignificant, but it is the lifeline of Palestinian families. We slept hungry, my siblings and I, with empty pots. My mother would distribute one piece of bread to each of us, just enough to keep us alive.

The doors of life closed on us. Instead of sitting in classrooms like other children around the world, we stood in lines at charity kitchens to secure a meal and struggled to find water, which became one of our biggest concerns.

One of us stood at the charity kitchen, another fetched water, and so our days passed.

Our dreams and childhood innocence were shattered. Who could have imagined that one day those laughs would disappear, and the purity of childhood would crumble before it even began?

We grew up too fast, yet we thank Allah for His countless blessings.

Standing at the door of our tent, I would look to the sky and ask:

Will we ever be like the rest of the children in the world?

Will we live in safety and peace, in a warm shelter to protect us? These are the simplest rights of life.

Date of Writing the Story: 2025/05/07

Doha Jafar Al-Omrani

Age: 44 years

My name is Doha Al-Omrani, from Gaza, the land of wars, blood, death, hunger, poverty, and blockade. We lack peace and security. We suffer from hunger, poverty, siege, and the high cost of living. After so many displacements, we now struggle with a lack of water, especially potable water when it's available.

We don't eat healthy food; what little we consume barely satisfies hunger. It's the same meager portions every day. We live without purpose, education, or a future. I wish for death to escape this life. Truly, I am exhausted and have suffered immensely. Even my home, my safe haven, is gone. My school is destroyed, my bike is destroyed, everything is in ruins. Finally, I wish to leave this place for somewhere better, where there is safety and peace.

Date of Writing the Story: 2025/05/27

Ula Sami Qouta

Age: 25 years

I have two children. We were displaced to several areas, and in each place, we faced hunger, pain, poverty, insecurity, insects, mosquitoes, scorching summers, and flooding winters.

Those were difficult days. I was pregnant and couldn't bear it anymore, I had nothing to nourish my unborn child. Days and nights passed, and I couldn't find a single loaf of bread to quell my hunger.

On the day of childbirth, I couldn't deliver due to severe malnutrition, there was no energy left in me.

Thankfully, with Allah's mercy, I gave birth safely in the school during those tough times.

We couldn't afford diapers, milk, or food, not even a kilo of flour. Famine spread across Gaza, prices skyrocketed, and markets were empty except for wild herbs. My husband picked wild greens, washed them, and we ate them.

Date of Writing the Story: 2025/05/22

Hind Aaid Habboosh

Age: 30 years

Original Place: Beit Lahiya

I used to live in my house in Beit Lahiya. We fled on foot to KhanYounis, enduring countless hardships and tragedies, remaining patient and steadfast.

We couldn't find a loaf of bread to sustain us. In Gaza, we don't ask for vegetables, meat, dairy, or cheese, we only ask for bread.

I have three siblings, and I am the sole caregiver for them.

My mother traveled to the West Bank to treat my brother, who has terminal cancer. She cannot return because of the occupation's closure of crossings.

Every day, I cry from frustration, hunger, and the rising cost of living. I want my mother to return quickly to ease my responsibility toward my siblings.

My father was martyred before my eyes, a scene I will never forget for as long as I live.

I live in torment and can't bear it anymore.

Oh Allah, bring my mother back to help me care for my siblings.

Date of Writing the Story: 2025/05/19

Basent Mohammad Abu Ouda

Age: 55 years

I live in Gaza, where the skies never quiet from the sounds of bombs, planes, and drones.

We sleep to the sound of shelling and wake up to it every day. The worst days of my life were when we left our home and fled to areas the Israeli occupation claimed were "safe." We stayed in a school, but it wasn't safe at all.

We were displaced multiple times under the sounds of shelling, killing, and bombs.

When I returned to my house, it was gone, my neighborhood, my school, my small bicycle, all vanished.

Even now, I am still displaced, moving from one place to another.

I hope this nightmare ends today, not tomorrow.

Don't forget us, always stand with us.

I dream of leaving Gaza to continue my education, go to school, and visit amusement parks and playgrounds.

Yes, I love life.

Date of Writing the Story: 2025/05/06

Tala Ali Abdulaal

Age: 36 years

Journey Through Genocide and Ethnic Cleansing

At 6:30 AM, I was getting ready to go to work. I taught at the Happy Child Nursery when suddenly, rockets began firing from Gaza, and explosions echoed in every corner of the strip. Screams filled the air.

I asked my mother, "What is happening?"

She replied, "Don't worry," though her face was full of fear. I rushed to my father for reassurance.

Suddenly, we realized the war had begun. The army ordered us to evacuate southward.

We lived in Tuffah, and this was our first displacement.

We went south to Al-Maghazi, staying in a school by the road. On Salah al-Din Street, I saw martyrs and wounded lying on the ground. Never in my life had I seen such horrific scenes.

We stayed for two weeks as prices skyrocketed insanely. We were deprived of food and clean water. Hunger and war combined made life unbearably hard.

After a ceasefire, we returned to eastern Gaza, refusing displacement. Life improved slightly, and aid began to trickle in. But peace was short-lived. War resumed, fiercer than before. Again, we faced shortages of food and flour.

My father risked his life daily to fetch flour. When he returned with provisions, it felt like a holiday.

We moved repeatedly, from Al-Sha'af to Al-Azhar University, then to Jabalia Camp, Al-Sidra, Al-Katiba, and back to Al-Sha'af. My father vowed, "We won't flee south."

There is no power or strength except with Allah.

Date of Writing the Story: 2025/05/10

Karima Muslim Qouta

Age: 30 years

Original Place: Tuffah Neighborhood

Place of Displacement: Al-Nafak Area

We suffered extreme poverty, and after displacement, our suffering intensified with hunger, poverty, and constant instability. We lacked food, water, clothing, and blankets.

Displaced without covers, we faced continuous problems. Fear, disease, and lack of sleep plagued us. We woke to the sounds of rockets and explosions.

We had no tents, living instead in tattered shelters. Medicine was unavailable.

I felt immense sorrow for my family. Each time we fled, difficulties and tragedies multiplied. The pain we endured was unbearable for any human, child, woman, or elder.

Displacement feels like recurring death. We can no longer tolerate moving, but we are forced to endure it. Suffering, oppression, and pain are overwhelming.

We pray to Allah to grant us patience and mercy upon the people of Gaza, besieged by hunger, poverty, and freezing cold.

Now, I am displaced with my family, living under makeshift shelters on the pavement, unprotected from the cold or bombardment. We suffer daily from the sounds of explosions and constant fear, hoping for the war to end.

Date of Writing the Story: 2025/05/03

Majda Al-Abd Abu Sukran

Age: 47 years

Profession: Social Researcher

On October 7th, we fled from our home in Shuja'iyya to my brother's house in Al-Sha'af, where we stayed for about nine days. Then, we fled to my aunt's house on Al-Mahkama Street for a month. During that time, we suffered from a lack of food and water, sharing a single loaf of bread among us. We ate just to survive.

Later, the occupation forces dropped leaflets ordering the evacuation of Shuja'iyya, which they subsequently destroyed completely, showing no regard for humans, stones, or trees.

The next day, we went to my brother's place near Al-Sayed Ali Mosque, where we stayed for a full month, moving around like nomads from one place to another. What a difficult life it was! Displacement is harder than death, death comes once, but displacement happens repeatedly.

Due to continuous shelling, we were displaced again to Mustaqbal School. On that day, the occupation bombed the school with a missile, and I witnessed the martyrs being torn apart, a scene I will never forget. By Allah's grace, we survived.

Afterward, we fled to Al-Shifa Hospital, which the occupation forces besieged. We couldn't even find a loaf of bread. The children screamed and cried from hunger, and we searched everywhere for a cup of water or a small piece of bread for my younger brother, but found nothing.

I don't know when this tragedy we are living through will end. No food, no water, no life… Allah is our only help.

Date of Writing the Story: 2025/05/07

Amal Yunis Abu Al-Darabi

Age: 39 years

Before the ominous October 7th, I lived a beautiful life. After that date, our lives were completely destroyed. In Beit Lahiya, we were displaced multiple times and nearly starved to death many times. In the north, we were besieged and couldn't even find a piece of bread. We searched everywhere for sustenance but found nothing. We ate tree leaves just to stay alive.

In Beit Lahiya, I often asked myself: Why can't we live like the rest of the world? Why can't we eat as they do? We longed intensely for vegetables, whose colors we had forgotten.

We fled to a school in Jabalia, which was later bombed. Both my husband and I suffer from heart disease, diabetes, and high blood pressure, and we were injured during the bombing of the school.

Then we fled south on foot, facing the occupation, fear, and hunger. I am sick, my husband is sick, and we lacked both medicine and food until we reached Deir Al-Balah.

We lived in a tent at a school, which was later bombed. Then we fled to Rafah.

Date of Writing the Story: 2025/05/19

Najla Majeed Rajeh

Age: 29 years

I lived with my husband in the Al-Sha'af area. On October 7th, at the start of the war, we fled to Abdul Fattah School. My youngest daughter suffered from malnutrition. We stayed in Gaza for five months, then fled to Mu'tasim School, returned to Abdul Fattah School, and finally fled to Rafah, facing difficulties along the way.

Later, we fled to Al-Nuseirat, where I gave birth to my son Mohammad, who now suffers from malnutrition. Then we returned to our beloved Gaza, to my husband's house, which was completely destroyed, while the malnutrition of my children continued.

Afterward, we fled to Al-Nafak area, where we now live in a tent in Al-Nafak, enduring all kinds of tragedies, hardships, and problems. My children continue to suffer from malnutrition and poverty.

Praise be to Allah in all circumstances, and Allah is sufficient for us, and He is the best protector.

Date of Writing the Story: 2025/05/07

Iman Asaad Ghabbin

Age: 38 years

Original Place: Beit Lahiya

Place of Displacement: Jabalia Camp

On October 7th, I was in my home in Beit Lahiya. We fled to Jabalia Camp and then to Al-Maghazi. Amid intense shelling, my daughter suffered spasms and could not be saved by the ambulance due to the severity of her condition.

Then we went to Mawasi in Rafah. Facing difficulties, the occupation issued an evacuation order for Rafah, so we fled to KhanYounis on the seashore. We stayed there for three months under hunger and siege, with nothing for our children to eat or drink.

Then we fled to Deir Al-Balah. We were exhausted from repeated displacements. Later, a ceasefire was announced, and we returned to our bombed house, setting up a tent over its ruins.

But the war resumed, and we fled again to Al-Nafak area.

Date of Writing the Story: 2025/05/07

Amal Khader Al-Hayya

Age: 47 years

It was a harsh day unlike any we had ever known, the seventh of October. On that Saturday morning, at exactly 6:25 AM, I was combing my daughter's hair, dressing my youngest child in his school uniform, and preparing breakfast for them and my husband before he left for work.

Suddenly, explosions erupted from every direction. At first, we didn't understand what was happening. I brought my children back inside, and after hours, we realized the magnitude of the event.

We spent only one night in our home in Shuja'iyya before missiles rained down upon us. We fled for the first time, and the beginning came, though the end has yet to arrive.

Our journey began at Al-Sabrah School, where we spent more than forty days filled with oppression, pain, and longing to return to our home and dreams. But we were forced to flee south with my children, leaving behind a piece of my heart, no, my entire heart, with my husband, who remained alone in Gaza due to circumstances beyond our control.

We crossed the barrier of death by Allah's grace, reaching a school in Al-Nuseirat for just one night. Then we moved to a school in KhanYounis, enduring twenty days of oppression. Afterward, we relocated to Rafah following the evacuation of KhanYounis.

Another school bore witness to our suffering, hunger, tears, anxiety, and above all, the pain of separation from my husband, the pillar of our family. Our children never stopped yearning for him and asking about him.

Finally, the day came. After five months of displacement from Rafah, resilience turned into homelessness once again, but this time, the tent carried the heaviest meanings of oppression, indescribable and unbearable.

We endured every kind of torment, and then fate delivered the hardest blow to my heart: death.

Like thunder, the news of my beloved husband's martyrdom struck my heart. It was like a lightning bolt I refused to accept. His heart could not believe it because hours before his martyrdom, he had been making preparations for us, bringing clothes, toys, food, and drinks for our children. He was eagerly awaiting the moment of reunion, but Allah willed otherwise, choosing him for the greatest meeting in Paradise.

And here I am today, back in Gaza, in the home Allah preserved for us, suffering from loss, pain, and loneliness. I relive painful memories, alone within the walls of my house.

This was not the end. I still flee with my children from one place to another, to Al-Tuffah, then to Al-Nafak, hoping to return to my home in Shuja'iyya.

Date of Writing the Story: 2025/05/09

Manar Nabil Al-Attar

Age: 36 years

On October 7th, I was in my home in Al-Attatra, Beit Lahiya. Afterward, we fled to schools in Gaza. In those schools, we witnessed with our own eyes the occupation bombing them, facing harsh and difficult conditions like hunger, destruction, fear, and oppression. Our children suffered deeply; some lost their hearing and speech.

We then fled to Deir Al-Balah on Salah Al-Din Street, staying in a residential school amidst heavy shelling. After confronting the enemy, we fled to Rafah, where we faced many difficulties, our children's hunger and our constant fear of ongoing bombardment.

Then we fled back to Deir Al-Balah, staying in another school and facing hardships both at the schools and on Salah Al-Din Street.

Later, we fled to the coastal area between Al-Maghazi and Al-Nuseirat, living in a tent and enduring many challenges. Our children experienced exhaustion, hardship, hunger, and pain.

Eventually, we returned to our beloved home in Beit Lahiya, but after a short while, the war resumed, and we fled again to Al-Nafak area.

Date of Writing the Story: 2025/05/09

Arifa Jihad Gaben

Age: 46 years

I am from the north, from Beit Lahiya, where hope melts away amidst overwhelming pain. On October 7th, we were forced to flee to escape relentless bombardment and hunger that drained our bodies and burdened our hearts. We yearned for the simplest necessities of life: food to satisfy us, water to quench our thirst, and safety to bring peace of mind.

We settled in a small tent, which was not just a shelter but a prison for us. In summer, the sun scorched us mercilessly, insects filled the space, and mosquitoes spread diseases without pause. When winter arrived, we didn't know whether to face freezing cold or floodwaters that submerged our tent, alongside overflowing sewage adding unbearable suffering.

We live a real tragedy, not knowing when it will end. We have no answer to the question: Will there come a day when this darkness lifts? Every passing day adds weight to the sorrow in our hearts, yet we cling to a glimmer of hope for a better tomorrow. How hard our lives are! And how cruel it is that hope remains all we have against these storms.

Date of Writing the Story: 2025/05/19

Khadija Mohammad Gaben

Age: 39 years

On October 7th, I stayed in my house, living somewhat peacefully until suddenly we heard loud explosions and shelling in Beit Lahiya. We fled to Al-Maghazi. Amidst intense shelling, we faced countless difficulties. We lived, yet we didn't truly live, we wished for death every moment. Why should we live when we cannot live like the rest of the world? We lack security and safety and crave food; we don't eat. Children scream from hunger and stand in long lines at charity kitchens hoping for a plate of lentils, mujadara, or rice. After hours of waiting, they often leave empty-handed. Our days revolve around running from place to place to secure a piece of bread for the children. One day, unable to find fresh bread, I soaked dry bread in water and fed it to my children and myself.

Date of Writing the Story: 2025/05/04

Samira Khaled Qouta

Age: 44 years

Before October 7th, we lived a beautiful life. We went to school and work, enjoying a calm and happy existence. We ate and drank, relishing chicken, vegetables, cheese, tea, and coffee.

Now, our situation brings tears even to stones before humans, there's nothing to eat; everything is unavailable.

We don't want to live as others do worldwide; we only wish to remain steadfast in this difficult and bitter life.

I don't know what sin Gaza's children committed to be deprived of Allah's blessings. It breaks my heart to see what has become of them.

Date of Writing the Story: 2025/05/08

Baraa Tawfiq Abu Darabi

Age: 30 years

I have two children. We lived in Beit Lahiya like other residents of Gaza, eating, drinking, and living safely. Then came October 7th, the ominous day, I don't know why it came or what sin we committed to deserve punishment. We were displaced multiple times, enduring suffering, homelessness, oppression, pain, and darkness.

One day, the occupation bombed the neighboring house and threw gas bombs, causing my family to suffocate. I saw martyrs flying through the air, women and men running in the streets in horror. Afterward, we decided to flee to Al-Jalaa Street, grateful for escaping safely despite leaving behind our belongings, clothes, and food. We fled barefoot from death. We spent an entire night on the street, then headed to the checkpoint and walked to Mawasi Khan Yunis because we had no money for transportation. There, we lived in a hallway inside a school since there was no room in classrooms or courtyards, and we couldn't afford a small tent. Those were the hardest days of my life, I wished for death, hoping to find solace in it.

Afterward, we began the torment of hunger, a pain no one can describe. My children screamed, not asking for chicken or meat like other children worldwide but simply begging for a loaf of bread. Can the world believe that our true demand is just a loaf of bread?

Later, we returned to Gaza, to Al-Nafak area, facing many hardships, tragedies, hunger, oppression, destruction, and fear. Allah is sufficient for us, and He is the best protector.

Date of Writing the Story: 2025/05/11

Samar Nahed Abu Darabi

Age: 37 years

I lived in Beit Lahiya. On October 7th, we fled to Al-Fakhoura School, then to Al-Muaskar School, where we stayed for two months. From there, we moved to Abu Hussein School, staying another two months. Then we fled to Deir Al-Balah, where my husband sustained war injuries. I stayed with him for two weeks in Nasser Hospital under critical conditions. Afterward, we fled to Mawasi Khan Yunis.

When the ceasefire was announced, we returned to Gaza, to Beit Lahiya. But the war resumed, forcing us to flee again, to Beit Hanoun, then to Tamraz Station, where we faced immense difficulties, tragedies, hunger, oppression, destruction, and fear. Praise be to Allah in all circumstances, and Allah is sufficient for us, and He is the best protector.

Date of Writing the Story: 2025/04/05

Afnan Ashraf Al-Sayyis

Age: 38 years

Our suffering began on October 7th after the Israeli occupation forces warned Gaza and its northern areas, forcing residents to flee south under threats of tanks and random shelling. It was a day of hardship unlike any we'd known before.

On Saturday morning at 6 AM, explosion sounds erupted everywhere. Initially, we didn't understand what was happening, but after hours, the truth dawned upon us.

We spent one night in our home in Shuja'iyya, a night no one anticipated. Rockets were launched, and killing and destruction began. We fled for the first time to my parents' home in Al-Zaytoun, shocked deeply by the first day of displacement.

My husband and I were there when a nearby house was bombed, triggering screams, fear, and the extraction of martyrs. We stayed about a month at my parents' home.

Later, surrounding areas were threatened, so we fled to Al-Sabrah School, spending a week on the roof amid cold winds and planes. The school was besieged, bullets flew toward us, and fear intensified. With great difficulty, we escaped and were forced to flee south.

The shock deepened when news reached us of a house being completely destroyed, it was Allah's will. We crossed the barrier of death miraculously, reaching a school in Al-Nuseirat, where we stayed for one night. Then we moved to Khan Yunis, enduring twenty bitter days.

We later relocated to Rafah after Khan Yunis was evacuated. Another school witnessed hunger, pain, oppression, fear, and above all, the anguish of separation from my family: my father, mother, and siblings.

After five months of displacement, homelessness struck again. The most devastating news reached my heart, the martyrdom of my younger brother. It felt like lightning striking my soul. He was my support and beloved, yet I couldn't bid him farewell due to the occupation.

Afterward, we fled to a tent, suffering greatly and lacking treatment. My husband, diabetic, endured prolonged periods without medication, suffering indescribable pain.

Now, after patience and perseverance, I've returned to my family, whom Allah preserved for me. Yet, I grieve the loss of my brother and home. I settled in a tent in Shuja'iyya's streets, but displacement persists. I fled to Al-Zaytoun, staying there for two weeks, and now I'm in Al-Sahaba area in a tent, hoping to return and stabilize.

Date of Writing the Story: 2025/05/22

Zainab Asaad Suboh

Age: 39 years

My husband has a disability in his legs, and I suffer from a foot impairment. On October 7th, we fled from our home in Beit Lahiya to Jabalia's Hafsa School. We left with nothing, fleeing as disabled individuals needing assistance. We walked south to a school in Deir Al-Balah, then narrowly escaped when the school was bombed and fled to Rafah.

In Rafah, we lived in a tent, suffering from merciless hunger, fear, and pain while needing medical treatment. When Rafah was threatened, we fled on foot despite our disabilities, walking with hearts full of fear, hunger, pain, and oppression. We went to Deir Al-Balah, staying in a tent where hunger became our greatest concern. A loaf of bread symbolized an irreplaceable treasure for Palestinian families. Yes, it was the loaf of bread.

When the ceasefire was announced, we returned to our cherished Gaza, to our home in Beit Lahiya, but found only memories of it. We pitched a tent over our destroyed house, which became our sole refuge. Then the war returned fiercer than before, and here we are again enduring displacement and homelessness, now in a tent in Al-Nafak area.

Date of Writing the Story: 2025/05/17

Safaa Habib Al-Attar

Age: 38 years

Original Place: Al-Attatra

Place of Displacement: Al-Sahaba

On October 7th, I was in my home in Al-Attatra, Beit Lahiya. When the shelling and displacement began, we moved to An-Nasr School, where we stayed for a long time. We faced immense difficulties, hunger and fear. The school was bombed, forcing us to flee again to Deir Al-Balah.

In Deir Al-Balah, we lived in another school. I was sick, and my husband was with me. We suffered greatly from hunger and fear. There, I lost my children, whom I had raised with love and hope in Egypt.

We later fled to Rafah, living in a small tent, enduring the biting winter cold and scorching summer heat. Above all, hunger was the cruelest challenge. We couldn't even find a loaf of bread, the lifeline of Palestinian families, and some days, we found none at all.

At times, we resorted to eating tree leaves or barley, using pasta as a flour substitute. Our dreams became exceedingly simple, all we wished for was a single loaf of bread.

When the ceasefire was announced, we returned to our home, now reduced to mere memories. We rejoiced briefly, thanking Allah for keeping us alive, but our joy was incomplete as the war resumed with greater ferocity.

Once again, we fled our land, heading to Al-Sahaba area, where we currently reside in a small tent. Praise be to Allah, Lord of the Worlds, for keeping us alive and giving us hope for a better future.

Date of Writing the Story: 2025/05/08

Jinat Mohammad Abdulaal

Age: 33 years

Since the start of the Al-Aqsa Flood Uprising on October 7, 2023, Gaza has faced unimaginably difficult days for all its residents, young and old, men and women. In this year, and in the years that followed, many have been martyred, injured, or displaced, and to this day, people continue to suffer from injuries, martyrdom, and displacement.

Displacement in Gaza means preserving life while fearing for our children, fleeing and becoming scattered from one place to another, and living in fear, even of stray dogs. We endured displacement, accepted the pain of living in tents, and bore it with patience.

But what we couldn't endure was hunger, the greatest of our pains. I cried day and night as I watched my siblings starve to death and my father struggle with despair because he couldn't provide even a piece of bread for his children.

We forgot the meaning of words like "fruit," "vegetables," and "meat." Every day, we stood in line at charity kitchens, hoping to get food. Sometimes I returned home with a small bowl of rice, and other times I came back empty-handed.

We slept with empty stomachs. If bread was available, it was divided among us, one loaf shared by me and my siblings just to stay alive.

I dreamed of being like other children in the world one day, playing and laughing without worrying about how or where to find our next meal.

When we returned to our homes, we found them reduced to rubble. Praise be to Allah for everything. The war resumed again, and now I pray for it to end so we can live in peace.

Date of Writing the Story: 2025/05/07

Sahar Nahid Abu Darabi

Age: 44 years

On October 7th, I was getting my daughters ready to go to school when suddenly we heard loud explosions, gunfire, and clashes, our house is very close to the border. On the first day, we fled to a school in Jabalia Camp, where we stayed for over a month and a half. One day, food and flour prices skyrocketed in the north, making the situation unbearable, so we fled south.

I fled with my seven daughters, leaving my husband behind. It was incredibly difficult, especially under constant shelling and fear. As we fled, bombs rained above us and bodies lay beneath our feet along Salah al-Din Street. A week later, my husband joined us in the south. From there, we fled to Deir al-Balah, staying at Al-Mazra'a School, where we were besieged for more than ten days.

After five months, we moved to Rafah, then returned to Deir al-Balah, pitching a tent near the beach. My daughters fell ill from the cold weather, and we suffered from hunger, eating moldy flour. We ate only one meal a day due to the severe food shortage. I was pregnant but miscarried due to the harsh conditions.

Later, we walked back to our beautiful hometown. But the war returned, and now we live in a tent in Al-Nafak area. I hope this war ends so we can live in peace.

Date of Writing the Story: 2025/04/04

Tahrir Saleh Al-Attar

Age: 36 years

I lived in Beit Lahiya. On October 7th, due to intense shelling and fear, we fled to Gaza New School. The school and the nearby tower were bombed, and my husband was injured in his left hand. Then we fled to Salah al-Din Street, where we stayed for seven hours before heading south to a residential school. There, we faced immense difficulties: lack of money, food, and hunger. My husband's hand bled due to the lack of medical treatment.

We were trapped in the school for three days amid heavy gunfire. Eventually, we fled on foot to Rafah, carrying our two children and my injured husband. We pitched a tent near the Egyptian wall and stayed for three months until Israeli forces entered Rafah, ordering evacuation under the pretext of protection and bringing food and water. When we exited the building, they deceived us, taking the men and leaving the women.

After two days, my husband and brother returned wearing women's clothes after being interrogated. They were released after confirming no suspicions against them. Ten minutes later, Israeli forces opened fire on us; out of twelve men, only four survived, including my husband and brother.

The joy of my children seeing their father and uncle alive was immense. Afterward, we fled to Tel Shomer School, where tanks surrounded the schools and bombs fell above us. Despite the danger, I felt some stability being in a classroom with two other families.

Eventually, we fled to my brother-in-law's house in the south for a month. At that time, Israeli forces set up checkpoints. Fearing arrest at the checkpoint, my husband hesitated to cross, but I reassured him. Despite threats and leaflets dropped by the occupation, we crossed but, unfortunately, they took my husband.

It was a heartbreaking day for me and my children. Life without him was extremely difficult, and I suffered greatly.

Date of Writing the Story: 2025/05/07

Mona Fadi Gaben

Age: 39 years

On October 7th, we fled – I, my husband, and our children – to my parents' house. My sister-in-law was injured in her leg, and as the shelling intensified, we fled to Tal al-Rabie School, settling into a classroom shared by seven families. Later, the occupation issued an immediate evacuation order, which we ignored. They bombed the school, killing residents inside. In terror, everyone fled south, but I went to my sister-in-law's house in Jabalia.

From there, we fled to schools in the camps, setting up a tent in the hallway of a school with my husband, children, sick mother, and sister whose leg had been amputated in 2009. The occupation bombed the school bathrooms, forcing us to flee east. Hours later, we realized we were surrounded. People began contacting relatives, warning them to leave immediately. As people tried to escape, Israeli soldiers fired on them, some were killed, others injured, and no one could save them.

It was a horrifying and terrifying day. We recited our final prayers, crying as we witnessed the wounded pleading for help. Ambulances arrived, but Israeli forces shot at them too, forcing them to retreat while the victims bled to death.

For ten days, we survived on salty water until the occupation claimed they wanted to protect us and bring food. Once outside, they deceived us, taking the men and leaving the women. Two days later, my husband and brother returned after interrogation, having been tortured and stripped of their clothes.

Despite everything, my children were overjoyed to see their father and uncle alive. We then fled to Tel Shomer School, enduring bombings and witnessing martyrs daily. Afterward, we moved to Shadia Abu Ghazala School in Jabalia, where we stayed the longest despite constant shelling.

Finally, we fled to my brother-in-law's house in the south. Crossing the checkpoint was perilous, but I insisted we proceed. Although they threatened us with leaflets and bombed houses, we managed to cross, but tragically, they took my husband. Life without him was unbearably hard, but we endured.

Date of Writing the Story: 2025/05/07

Marwa Hekmat Gaben

Age: 47 years

I am from the north, from Beit Lahiya in the Sultan area. On October 7th, I fled to Sheikh Radwan, staying for a week, then to a school for a month. We were besieged for three days without water, and the school was bombed. My daughter suffocated from tear gas, and we narrowly escaped.

We went to Shadia Abu Ghazala School, staying for two weeks, but were forced to flee again to Shuja'iyya, where my husband was martyred. The occupation destroyed Shuja'iyya, so we returned to Shadia Abu Ghazala School, only for it to be bombed again. We fled west to Wazir School, where famine struck alongside shortages of medicine.

My daughter suffered hunger, deprivation, and the loss of her father, as well as lingering effects from the gas. We returned to Shuja'iyya for a month, then fled south to Rafah to feed my youngest child. We stayed at Kamal Adwan School, then moved to Khan Yunis. Afterward, we returned north following a ceasefire, but the war resumed, forcing us to flee to Al-Sahaba area.

I pray this will be our last displacement. Praise be to Allah, Lord of the Worlds.

Date of Writing the Story: 2025/04/04

Marwa Hekmat Gaben

Age: 49 years

Before October 7th, we lived peacefully in Beit Lahiya. That day, we fled to Hafsa School in Jabalia, where the Israeli occupation bombed us five times. We fled to Palestine School, then returned to Hafsa. On February 12th, the school was bombed, and my cousin's son was martyred before our eyes. On March 12th, we fled to Abu Zaytoun School during a stormy, rainy night, taking only the clothes on our backs. Our children suffered from hunger and cold, and that night remains etched in history for its brutality.

We returned to Hafsa, enduring famine and hardship. One day, my son cried, "Mom, I'm hungry." I made him the last bit of pasta we had, shedding tears as I prepared it. For days, we fasted so I could save food for my children.

On May 3rd, we fled south to Mazra'a School. Along the way, we saw tanks, soldiers, and bodies littering the ground. We stayed there for five months, then moved to Deir al-Balah, and finally to the beach. Unable to endure life by the sea, we returned to the school.

Later, we fled to Al-Nuseirat, where famine and suffering returned stronger than ever. During the ceasefire, we returned north, grateful despite the destruction and hunger. Forty days later, the war resumed, and we fled to Al-Nafak, pitching a tent under a bombed building. The massacres and famine worsened.

Date of Writing the Story: 2025/04/06

Fida Habib Al-Attar

Age: 39 years

I lived in my home in Al-Attatra, Beit Lahiya. On October 7th, we fled to a school in An-Nasr, facing numerous challenges: fear, hunger, and anxiety. Then we fled south, living in a tent. Our financial situation was dire, with widespread famine and shortages of food and water. My husband, unable to work due to illness, struggled alongside us.

Desperate, I decided to build a clay oven to bake bread, providing meals for my children and others in the camp. By Allah's grace, we earned a small income that sufficed for our daily needs. When the ceasefire came, we returned home, only to find it completely destroyed. Undeterred, we built another tent and constructed another clay oven. Praise be to Allah for everything.

Date of Writing the Story: 2025/05/02

Duaa Hamza Qouta

Age: 39 years

Our family consists of six members: three sons, a daughter, and my husband and me. We lived humbly in Gaza City's Al-Sha'af neighborhood, thanking Allah for His blessings. We were displaced multiple times and spent a long period in a tent at Al-Shifa Hospital.

The hardest days came when the occupation besieged Al-Shifa. We endured unimaginable hardships, unable to find even a small piece of bread to quiet our children's hunger. We ate tree leaves and drank undrinkable water. We witnessed the occupation destroy Al-Shifa, humiliate doctors, and arrest them. Martyrs fell everywhere, and women screamed in anguish.

Despite all this, we persevered for the sake of our children, entrusting our suffering to Allah.

We ask for your prayers for us and the beloved people of Gaza. May Allah have mercy on the martyrs, heal the wounded, and relieve our burdens and those of all Muslims.

Date of Writing the Story: 2025/05/08

Ruzan Mansour

Age: 20 years

Original Place: Gaza

Place of Displacement: Khan Yunis

From Bliss to Hell

On October 7th, we woke up to the sounds of rockets coming from every direction. We lived near the border, close to the eastern line of Al-Shuja'iyya neighborhood. In a rush, we gathered some belongings and fled our home, leaving behind everything we cherished, our house, memories, and beloved possessions.

Our family consists of nine members: my mother, father, five sons, and two daughters. We stepped out into the street, unsure of where to go or what was happening. Later, we learned that the Palestinian resistance had stormed Israeli settlements, capturing many soldiers. The bombardment on the entire Gaza Strip was relentless and intense.

We sought refuge at a relative's house, staying there for about a week. Then came the orders to evacuate northern Gaza and head south. My father owned a car, so we packed our belongings, got in, and drove south. Upon arrival, we found ourselves stranded in the streets, unsure of what to do next. We eventually found a nearby camp and moved in. There, we endured the summer heat, insects, contagious skin diseases, and shortages of food, clean water, and medicine. Securing basic necessities became a major challenge.

Later, we moved to another camp in Rafah, facing the same struggles: lack of food and water, with no basic amenities available.

My parents are the heroes of this sorrowful tale.

My beloved father always protected us, doing everything he could to keep us safe.

My dear mother cooked for us, consoled us, and eased the burden of these difficult days. Our family was beautiful, filled with love and affection.

We then moved to a school in Khan Yunis. My father, who was educated and worked as an accountant at a bank, was offered a position in the administration upon our arrival. He kindly accepted. Our living conditions improved; trucks began arriving, goods became available, and life seemed easier. Despite losing our three-story home to bombing, we still clung to hope of returning to Gaza.

After weeks, we received news that we would be allowed to return. We drove back in our car, and my father pointed out familiar places along the way. To our astonishment, nothing remained as it was. When we arrived, we found no place to live. After a long search, we rented an apartment in Jabalia, where we stayed for about a month. My family was happy because it reminded us of our lost home. Though we felt safe and stable, my father wasn't comfortable with the apartment and kept urging his friends to find us a better place.

Ramadan came, and we welcomed it with joy. I spent some of the happiest days with my family until that fateful day...

We were awake for Suhoor. My father sat with us while my mother prepared food in the kitchen. Suddenly, the sound of rockets filled the air, intense and overwhelming. My mother gathered us in one spot, as she always did during wars, ready to face whatever might come.

My father got up to perform ablution. We begged him to leave the house, terrified. He replied, "Caution does not prevent fate." Then he went to wash. When we insisted again, he said, "Nothing will happen to us except what Allah has decreed."

Suddenly, I found myself buried under rubble, surrounded by darkness, stones, and dust. I couldn't see or hear anything. Where were my siblings? Who survived? Who didn't? I lay unconscious for a long time.

Rescue teams eventually pulled me out first and rushed me to the nearest hospital. I repeatedly asked, "What happened to my family?" No one answered.

They brought my other siblings to the same hospital. I froze when I saw my mother lying motionless, with my younger brother and sister beside her. Time seemed to stop; I couldn't process what I was seeing.

My beloved mother had passed away.

My innocent younger siblings were gone too.

I cried endlessly, heartbroken. I thought, *When I see my father, I'll hug him and tell him everything.*

But hours passed, and my father never came. Relatives arrived to bury my mother and siblings, while we waited for news of him. After a long wait, we learned that my father had also been martyred.

Our peace was stolen, our safety shattered.

My dear father, the pillar of our family, our first love, and a man of good memory, had left us in this fleeting world.

Mother, Father, Siblings, they were all gone forever.

Now, at such a young age, I carry this pain alone. I must stand strong for my remaining siblings. But no matter what I do, I can never replace what they've lost.

Date of Writing the Story: 2025/05/07

Weaam Nahed Weshah

Age: 38 years

I have four orphaned children.

I lived in Al-Shuja'iyya, Gaza, in a beautiful house we bought after much struggle, selling the car, gold, and borrowing money from relatives. My husband was a tailor.

Though life was modest, we were content. Every day at 4 PM, I eagerly awaited his return, bringing simple groceries like vegetables and sweets. Those were beautiful days despite their simplicity, and we lived peacefully.

This continued until October 7th, marking the worst days of my life. From the war's first day, we were displaced between shelters and relatives' homes.

The suffering intensified when a house nearby was completely bombed. Displacement continued alongside hunger. Flour disappeared from markets, and finding even a grain felt like discovering treasure. One day, my husband heard about flour trucks arriving at the Kuwaiti Roundabout. He joined a group of young men to fetch a bag of flour, but it turned out to be a trap set by Israeli forces. They waited until the youths gathered, then unleashed artillery fire, killing them all. This massacre became known as the Kuwait Massacre on January 25, 2024.

Our provider, my husband, was gone. His death left us with new hardships: displacement, homelessness, hunger, and loss.

While fleeing through narrow alleys, my eldest son, aged 10, was shot in the leg by a quad bike patrol.

Date of Writing the Story: 2025/05/11

Rana Rafeeq Rajeh

Age: 39 years

I lived in my husband's house near Ammar bin Yasir Mosque. On October 7th, I was forced to flee to a house on Salah al-Din Street, where I faced numerous challenges.

We endured hunger and fear in Gaza while many fled south. I stayed resilient in Gaza until I had to move to Al-Hasil area near Rashad Shawa Center.

Later, I moved again to the Industrial Zone with my husband and his family.

Then came the devastating news: my husband was martyred. May Allah grant him Paradise.

He left behind a child yet to be born, who entered this world as an orphan without ever seeing his father.

Date of Writing the Story: 2025/05/20

Sama Mohammad Al-Sa'idi

Age: 30 years

Profession: School Janitor

On the morning of October 7th, I woke up to go to work as a janitor at my school. Suddenly, I heard explosions launched by the occupying forces against Gaza City. These attacks were violent, resulting in massacres, death, and destruction.

I returned home crying, hugged my children, and wept together.

Later that night, at 11 PM, the occupation bombed my neighbor's house. I rushed out only to find my two friends torn apart, nothing remained but their hair. Their bodies had vaporized and fragmented.

It was an unimaginably painful sight.

Soon after, the occupation ordered Gaza residents to evacuate, directing us to southern areas they claimed were safe.

We left and spent our first night sleeping in the street. After two days outdoors, a school sheltered us. We set up tents between classrooms, enduring long lines for bathrooms, clean water, and food from charity kitchens.

One day, my neighbor Um Ihab and I went to fetch clean water. After hours, on our way back, the occupation bombed us. Um Ihab was killed instantly, leaving behind only her foot. It was a horrifying scene I'll never forget, watching her disintegrate into pieces before my eyes.

By Allah's grace, I narrowly escaped death.

We've grown old amidst constant death and bloodshed in the streets.

Return our home, return Gaza, bring back Umm Mohammad and Umm Ahmad, restore my happiness…

I won't recount the losses, deprivation, and war, it's been covered extensively in media. Yet, our reality is far worse.

I'm exhausted. Yes, truly exhausted. Where do we go? What's next?

Allah is sufficient for us, and He is the best protector.

Inas Mohammad Al-Halooli

Age: 55 years

What a devastating shock! How does it begin? How does it end? Pain and suffering.

Since the war began on October 7th, we've suffered immensely. We fled our home in Al-Shuja'iyya, moving first to my parents' house with my children, then to my brother's house in Rimal. Conditions worsened, and the shelling intensified.

We fled to Al-Nasser Children's Hospital, staying there for two days. Then my husband asked, "Do you want to leave for the south?"

We traveled to a UNRWA school called Abu Humais, located in Al-Bureij Camp. We stayed there from November to December, experiencing both joy and anguish. As the shelling increased, we fled again, from Al-Bureij to Rafah, settling in an area called Al-Shaer.

We ate, drank, cooked, and lived through both sweet and bitter moments.

Of course, the children didn't understand whether this situation was right or wrong, why they left their homes, or when they'd return.

There were many joyful moments, but also countless heartbreaking ones. We grieved being separated from our homes, lands, schools, mosques, trees, oranges, olives, and palms.

Months passed in this transient life until Rafah faced the threat of a ground invasion, prompting people to flee once more.

Finally, we reached Al-Nuseirat, where we now reside in Souq Balata, hoping to return safely to our homes.

Date of Writing the Story: 2025/05/06

Marwa Mohammad Al-Hawiti

Age: 50 years

I've spent my entire life amidst wars. Just as one ends, another begins. But this war is unlike any other, it's genocide, killing millions and displacing thousands. We've moved repeatedly from one place to another.

The occupation committed horrific massacres in Sheikh Radwan. We fled without any means of survival, moving to Al-Nuseirat, where kind souls sent us clothes. Then we relocated to a UNRWA clinic.

On Saturday, June 7, 2024, the occupation targeted prisoners, killing 200 martyrs and injuring many more. By Allah's mercy, we narrowly escaped.

I pray for the war to end and for us to return to our homes and beloved Gaza, which has been taken from us. We've endured 11 months of torment and destruction. Isn't that enough suffering?

Enough, world! We're tired, our patience is depleted, but Allah is with us, and we await His relief.

Date of Writing the Story: 2025/05/15

Israa Adel Al-Sa'idi

Age: 21 years

I woke up with my children to the sound of explosions launched by the brutal occupation against the city. These attacks were violent, resulting in massacres, and marking the beginning of death and destruction.

Later, the occupation ordered the residents of Gaza to evacuate the area, so we headed to "Al-Nasr," my family home. After a while, Al-Nasr was evacuated, leaving only me, my family, and my parents behind.

During repeated bombings in the area, my mother and brother were injured, so we fled to Al-Shifa Hospital. We were surrounded by tanks and artillery at Al-Shifa, so we decided to head south, believing it to be safer.

We fled on foot through what is called "Al-Hilaba," walking long distances from Al-Shifa to Rafah, not knowing where to go next. With no house to shelter us in the freezing cold, I set up a tent made of wood and blankets to keep us warm. My children and I suffered greatly from the cold.

This is my reality, and the reality of all displaced people. We endured water shortages, skyrocketing prices, epidemics, diseases, and heavy rains.

We were then ordered to evacuate again, so we moved to Al-Nuseirat Camp, where we stayed for two months. The camp was bombed, but by Allah's grace, we survived, though my uncle was martyred.

We fled to another tent. When summer arrived, we suffered immensely from the intense heat, insect infestations, and diseases.

O Allah, mend our situation, forgive us, and count us among the martyrs.

Date of Writing the Story: 2025/05/17

Amira Akram Al-Sa'idi

Age: 40 years

On the morning of October 7th, my four children and I woke up to the sound of violent explosions launched by the brutal occupation against the city. These attacks were devastating, causing massacres and widespread death and destruction.

Later, the occupation ordered the residents of Gaza to evacuate and head south, claiming it was safe.

My children and I fled without knowing where to go. Leaving Al-Shuja'iyya, we headed to Rafah, but we couldn't find a house to shelter us in the freezing cold. So, we set up a tent made of wood and blankets to protect us from the cold. My children and I suffered greatly.

This was our situation, and the situation of all displaced people. We faced water shortages, rising prices, outbreaks of disease, and heavy rains that worsened our suffering.

We were then ordered to evacuate again, so we moved to Al-Nuseirat Camp, where living conditions deteriorated further. Our daily routine became waiting in long lines for water, which barely sufficed to feed my children, and trying to adapt to these dire circumstances devoid of safety.

One early morning, a neighbor's house in Al-Nuseirat was bombed, killing eight people, mostly children and women. The explosion was so close that glass shattered, and many displaced people were injured. The place filled with screams, terror, and fear. I gathered my children and hugged them tightly. My son screamed, "Don't worry, don't worry, they hit the solar panels!" because he saw fragments of solar panels flying. Young men and security forces shouted, "They hit the solar panels!" This reassured me and eased my fear, calming both me and my children.

Minutes later, we went to the site, which was covered in rubble. But, thank Allah, the people and neighbors who were in the school survived, including my uncles and their children. Had the missile been slightly larger, the losses would have been catastrophic.

Every time I remember that day, I feel overwhelmed and lose control, thanking Allah countless times for sparing us from this massacre.

Date of Writing the Story: 2025/05/11

Zahra Ahmed Abu Kweik

On October 7th, a Saturday, I was sitting with my husband and children in the living room. Breakfast was prepared, and my children got ready for school. As for me, I was heading to the palm tree in our land to gather dates and eat them.

When I entered the house, Israeli bombings came from all directions, shocking us as we didn't know the reason. Later, we learned that the resistance had attacked Israeli soldiers and captured some, and we, being near the eastern border in Khazaa, were affected.

We left our house and went to Al-Mawasi, taking only two school bags with us. The locals were kind, and there was significant aid.

Afterward, we went to Rafah, where we set up a tent and stayed for three months. The heat was so intense that I couldn't fast during Ramadan.

Now, I pray to Allah to relieve our burdens, deliver us safely from this war, and reward us like those who persevere.

Date of Writing the Story: 2025/05/06

Aseel Mohammad Jouda

Age: 29 years

I am a girl from a simple family with old-fashioned values and complicated mindsets. I live in Jabalia Camp, where education is nearly nonexistent or impossible for most. However, I insisted on studying, and after much persistence, my family agreed.

On my first day of school, I was overjoyed, but my academic performance wasn't high due to the lack of supplies caused by harsh economic, social, and financial conditions.

Years passed until October 7th, the fateful day when our lives turned into pain, suffering, and oppression. Facing difficult circumstances, the hardest blow was being displaced to a tent, where life became unbearable.

A young man from the camp proposed to me, but I hesitated due to our dire situation. Eventually, I agreed to marry him, requesting to continue my studies afterward, a nearly impossible demand for his family.

I married against my will, leaving behind school, notebooks, books, and pens, entering a world I never imagined, one that distanced me from everything I loved.

Unfortunately, the marriage didn't last long, as our relationship became unbearable. Neither I nor my husband could tolerate each other, with problems escalating daily.

We suffered from pain, oppression, poverty, hunger, bombardment, and destruction.

Our marriage ended in divorce after several months, complicating matters further. Now, I endure war, pain, oppression, and divorce.

Allah is sufficient for us, and He is the best protector.

Salwa Jamal Abu Shaaban

Age: 38 years

Original Place: Tuffah Neighborhood

I was in my house in Arqam, Tuffah neighborhood, on October 7th, when we fled to a house in Al-Shuja'iyya with my in-laws.

I was terrified, as were my husband and family. I left my home without blankets, food, or clothes. My children are young, my husband is elderly, and I am pregnant.

I sat isolated in a room away from my in-laws, while my children felt fear and hunger due to water shortages and rising prices.

Later, I fled to a school, staying in a tent in the hallway without mattresses or blankets. I felt immense pain for my children, unable to provide them with food, clothes, or covers.

We suffered from a lack of drinking water and cleaning supplies.

Afterward, I fled to a school in Al-Zeitoun, facing repeated hardships: hunger, destruction, and overwhelming fear.

As a mother, I was deeply pained for my elderly husband, who was incapable of providing for our young children.

We endured hunger, pain, and fear, especially during the harsh winter.

We suffered from severe cold because my children are still very young.

How we endured hunger, fear, freezing cold, and rising prices in Gaza!

Date of Writing the Story: 2025/05/06

Amal Mosleh Rajeh

Age: 63 years

I lived in a simple house in Al-Sha'af neighborhood. On October 7th, we fled to schools, facing numerous difficulties: hunger, fear, destruction, overcrowded schools, and the challenges of living there.

We experienced the pain of hunger and longing for even the simplest food, a loaf of bread. Many people fled south due to food shortages, but despite the pain, fear, and hunger, both then and now, my family of seven struggled to find flour. High prices made it unaffordable.

My family and I prayed through fear, hunger, and hardship. How much I cried, and still cry. What else can I do?

Date of Writing the Story: 2025/05/19

Israa Moamen Rajeh

Age: 40 years

I lived in Al-Sha'af, around forty years old.

On October 7th, we fled to Abdul Fattah School with my family, father, and mother.

I went to Al-Nasser Hospital in Gaza, to the intensive care unit, where we were trapped amidst relentless shelling.

My parents suffered immensely.

We endured hunger in Gaza, where people were killed. My father was injured in his leg while trying to get a bag of flour.

My brother Mohammad joined us on January 7th during the war, witnessing our pain of hunger and fear alongside us.

Date of Writing the Story: 2025/04/28

Hayam Mahmoud Abu Hilima

Age: 30 years

Original Place: Beit Lahiya

Place of Displacement: Al-Shifa Hospital

I lived with my family in Beit Lahiya.

We fled to Al-Shifa Hospital, facing numerous hardships: poverty, famine, and skyrocketing prices. Flour became extremely expensive, making it unaffordable.

The lack of flour left us starving. Unable to buy bread, we resorted to eating animal feed, grinding and kneading it, and consuming herb leaves.

O Allah, ease our burdens.

Date of Writing the Story: 2025/05/24

Hanadi Abu Rashid

Age: 35 years

Original Place: Beit Lahiya

Place of Displacement: Deir Al-Balah

I am a mother of four children. This war taught me much about life's hardships, fear, hunger, and deprivation of basic necessities like food, clothing, and water.

At the start of the war, we fled to UNRWA schools, but due to intense shelling, we moved to my aunt's house in KhanYounis, staying for three days.

However, the bombing didn't stop. The occupation bombed our neighbor's house, and my children were terrified. At night, I took them to Nasser Hospital, where my father, Raddad, and Mohammad sustained head injuries from stress and fear.

Afterward, we fled to a school. Without blankets or mattresses, we slept on the ground. We then faced starvation, unable to feed my children for four months.

Later, KhanYounis was evacuated, and we fled again, my husband, children, and I, without taking anything with us.

We reached Deir Al-Balah, where we set up a tent that became the source of our greatest suffering. We endured hunger, pain, fear, and destruction.

Date of Writing the Story: 2024/08/07

Lina Habib Ghaben

Age: 35 years

Original Place: Beit Lahiya

Place of Displacement: Al-Naser Area

I have an injured husband and two children, a boy and a girl, and we live in Beit Lahiya.

On October 7th, our area was bombed, and at 3 PM, we fled to Gaza New Schools in Al-Nasr, where we stayed for a month and a half. During that time, the school was bombed, and my husband was injured in his left foot.

We then fled from the schools to the streets at night. I was five months pregnant.

We went to Sakeena School in Deir Al-Balah, where we were besieged for a week. Afterward, we fled to the beach, setting up a tent. There, we endured summer heat, winter cold, hunger, fear, oppression, and pain.

When a ceasefire was announced, we returned to our homes on foot, carrying my newborn child from this war.

But the war resumed, bringing displacement, fear, hunger, and homelessness once again.

Date of Writing the Story: 2024/05/14

Lina Saqer Qotah

Age: 20 years

Original Place: Al-Mashahira AreaPlace of Displacement: Al-Shuja'iyya

On October 7th, the cursed war began in Gaza. A week later, on October 15th, we fled to Al-Shuja'iyya neighborhood. After a month there, we moved south and stayed in KhanYounis for a month.

The pains of displacement multiplied; we never knew stability or safety during this war. We suffered greatly from a lack of food, water, and clothing, even something as simple as a loaf of bread was denied to us.

In this war, a loaf of bread became like a treasure and a source of happiness for us in Gaza.

What could we do?

We returned to our homes after the ceasefire, but the war, displacement, fear, and hunger returned once again. However, thank Allah, we are still in our home in Al-Mashahira, and I hope we don't have to flee again. Our greatest wish now is to stay in our homes, and we thank Allah for everything.

Date of Writing the Story: 2024/05/07

Suha Ayman Abu Dan

Age: 40 years

Original Place: RafahPlace of

Displacement: Mawasi, KhanYounis

We used to live in blessed Gaza, the land of olives and abundance. We were happy, we ate, cooked, and celebrated life. Suddenly, on October 7th, our lives were completely destroyed. Life lost all meaning.

We witnessed death more than once, endured immense suffering, and saw the most agonizing pain.

Every day brought us death, oppression, and sorrow, unforgettable and painful scenes. The martyrs became mere numbers in the register of pain.

The hardest part of this war was the spread of famine and poverty. There was no flour available, and if it was, it was too expensive for us to buy even a kilo.

We were forced to grind animal feed and eat weeds. Every day, we stood in long lines at charity kitchens, hoping to get a plate of lentils or rice.

They deprived us of everything, they deprived us of life.

Date of Writing the Story: 2025/05/07

Basma Yahya SaqerAge: 40 years

Original Place: KhanYounis

We lived in KhanYounis, owning farmland where we grew crops and ate. We never complained before.

I had four sons who studied, and after school, they helped their father with farming. We were happy, cooking, eating, and drinking, thanking Allah for everything.

Suddenly, life turned upside down, and my eldest son, Mohammad, was martyred.

Our dreams and hopes vanished, he was martyred right before my eyes.

What a difficult life this has become!

In addition to famine, poverty, and pain, the occupation destroyed our homes, razed our lands, and annihilated us. They killed our youth, and our lives have become an indescribable tragedy.

We can't find anything to eat or drink. We search all day at charity kitchens just to fill our stomachs. We can't even find a small piece of bread.

Allah is sufficient for us, and He is the best protector.

Date of Writing the Story: 2025/05/06

Majida Youssef Al-Sadiq

Age: 47 years

Original Place: Deir Al-Balah

Before October 7th, our lives were happy, everything was available: electricity, water, stability, and safety. We went on summer trips to the beach and prepared delicious meals in our beautiful homes, which had air conditioners that made life comfortable.

Suddenly, without any fault of ours, everything changed, and we lived the worst days of our lives. We fled from place to place, living in a small tent that didn't protect us from the summer heat or the freezing winter cold. We cooked over open fires, which caused several illnesses, and washed our clothes by hand.

We couldn't find anything to eat. Every day, we searched for food and water. We were deprived of vegetables, fruits, and even flour. Flour disappeared from the markets, and when it was available, it was outrageously expensive.

Despite all this, we accepted our fate, thanking Allah for everything.

Date of Writing the Story: 2025/04/03

Noor Rafiq Qotah

Age: 40 years

Original Place: Al-Daraj Neighborhood

I lived in my house with my sick husband, in a modest family. On the morning of October 7th, we were shocked by rockets falling on Gaza, and my family and I felt intense fear. Our lives were turned upside down.

We fled to schools seeking safety, where we faced numerous difficulties. We suffered from poverty, pain, oppression, hunger, and mounting debts. We had no clothes, food, or water, and we couldn't provide anything due to the continuous bombardment in our area.

In displacement, we suffered from a lack of food, especially flour, and a shortage of tents and blankets. Our children screamed from hunger, thirst, and the freezing cold at night, surrounded by darkness, ignorance, and a lack of education.

My husband suffers from a chronic illness and has undergone multiple surgeries. He struggled due to poor hygiene and malnutrition. We lived in a tent without a bathroom, deprived of privacy.

We have no solutions, we are utterly helpless, relying only on patience, trying to endure all this suffering.

Date of Writing the Story: 2025/04/24

Naeed Rashad Abu Shaqfa

Profession: English Teacher in Kindergarten

We lived a somewhat beautiful life despite the siege and hardships, but at least we had some stability.

Suddenly, our lives turned into unimaginable destruction, bombings, fire, humiliation, and loss of dignity. We were humiliated, truly humiliated.

Women, children, youth, and elders, all are suffering.

The occupation, which claims to be "the most ethical army," has neither ethics nor dignity. My house was bombed, and I couldn't take anything, not for myself, not for my husband, not for my children. Even my husband's car was gone, with it, our dreams, our future, everything.

Now we live in hunger, poverty, and thirst, homeless, waiting for evacuation orders at any moment. Neither the Zionists, nor the Arabs, nor foreigners care about us.

We are forgotten, as if we don't exist in anyone's calculations.

We want to eat.

We want to dream.

We just want to sleep one night without the sound of shelling.

My youngest son wakes up terrified from the sound of artillery fire.

Allah is sufficient for us, and He is the best protector.

Since October 7th until now, we've been suffering from displacement and the relentless sound of shelling. We see people torn apart, and many have lost their entire families...

All because of the world's silence on these massacres.

I don't know why all this hatred...

Allah is sufficient for us, and He is the best protector.

We've been displaced more than ten times, and every time, we pick ourselves up and start over: no clothes, no food, no water.

Date of Writing the Story: 2025/05/25

Salwa Zaki Abu Haloub

The war of October 7th came suddenly and destroyed our lives. We lived in a beautiful new house, and suddenly, the war took away everything precious.

Since the beginning of the war, we've been continuously displaced, moving from place to place, with nothing.

I was at Abu Hussein School when it was bombed. I was inside and had to flee, leaving my belongings behind.

Displacement was extremely hard for me because I have a disabled son, and I didn't have money to move south. My situation was incredibly difficult.

When the ceasefire came, we set up tents and lived in them, but then the war resumed, and we returned to displacement, starting over again from scratch.

Date of Writing the Story: 2025/05/23

Alaa Majed Al-Manasra

Age: 19 years

Original Place: Al-Shuja'iyya

Place of Displacement: Deir Al-Balah

The Story of Five Orphaned Sisters Facing the Horrors of War in a Displacement Tent

Ala' found herself responsible for her four younger sisters after their father was martyred. At just 19, she took on the role of a parent, shouldering immense responsibility.

Ala' constantly asks herself: Are we living a nightmare?

She found herself suddenly responsible for four younger sisters, living alone in a tent within an orphanage camp in Mawasi, KhanYounis.

Ala', now 19, wished this was merely a bad dream, hoping to wake up with her sisters back home with their father.

She was stunned to find herself an orphan, responsible for four younger siblings. "We need someone to care for us and protect us," she said.

Ala' and her sisters live in a tent after fleeing from Rafah, a journey filled with torment and cruelty. Their father used to care for them and handle every detail of their lives.

They moved to a shelter in a school, staying there for months.

One unforgettable day, Ala' witnessed the details of her father's martyrdom.

"He went to KhanYounis, promising to return quickly, but he never came back. We learned he was martyred and couldn't find his body despite searching for a long time. Witnesses told us the occupation killed him and buried him in a mass grave with other martyrs."

Their lives turned upside down, and Ala' found herself responsible for daily tasks like cleaning, washing, and providing food and water.

Despite the terrifying conditions of war, she cooperates with her sisters to bear these burdens. They rely heavily on charitable aid.

"I've come to realize this harsh reality," says Ala'. "Despite my young age, I understand my great responsibility."

The family depends on food provided by charity kitchens and cleans their sleeping areas inside the tent.

They eat whatever breakfast is available, then head to school, returning to the camp to search for lunch.

Ala' makes handmade crafts for girls and sells them in the camp to earn some money.

Each sister has her own wish, but they share one big dream: to reunite with their father.

Lina Al-Za'abootAge: 25 years

Where do I begin?

I'm Lina, some call me "Umm Mahmoud."

I graduated at 24. How old do you think I am now? If you saw me, you'd think I'm 30, though I haven't yet turned 25.

Do you want to hear my story? Open my palm and look at the map drawn by the occupation. Don't be afraid, my friend, this blackness etched on my hand isn't a disease; it's the scars of fire and smoke. Do you think it only consumed my hand? It entered my chest, tightening around my neck. I have a heart condition that can't tolerate smoke. Do you think it's just cooking smoke? No, my friend, it's the smoke from rockets and artillery that strained my hearing and raised my blood pressure. Are my eyes tearing up? Do you think they're crying over that? No, my friend.

My tears fall for my child, who hasn't yet reached four years old, for every tremble in his hands and every jolt in his heart.

Mahmoud, my eldest son, gathers firewood from the streets. Do you think I'm joking?

Since that day, after October 7th, every fiery belt carved itself into our hearts, displacing us and forcing us to flee to a school. In that corner of the classroom, I'll never forget! The cold devoured our bodies without blankets or sleep.

How could I forget my mother's trembling hands? Or my father's eyes? Or my sister's children? Or my brother, who stripped off all his clothes to warm my son? Time passes, and we wait for that dream we still hope for, to see the end of the war!

Doha Rafiq Rajeh

Age: 30 years

Original Place: Al-Shuja'iyya

Place of Displacement: Al-Tuffah Neighborhood

I lived in a simple house with my family, and we had already been struggling with poverty before October 7th.

On October 7th, my family and I were shocked by the missiles raining down on us and the sound of explosions. We fled our home to Al-Tuffah in Gaza, leaving behind food, drink, and even clothing.

We suffered deeply, feeling fear, hunger, and immense pain. Then we fled to schools, where we endured excruciating suffering from hunger, thirst, fear, cold, and a lack of medical treatment and water.

Later, the occupation dropped leaflets, so we fled to Al-Rimal. Our suffering was indescribable, and our dignity was wounded. Debts piled up, and we faced countless problems. The word "displacement" became our greatest burden, moving from one place to another.

With every displacement, we faced the same pains: hunger, oppression, fear, agony, and deprivation. We were denied safety and the simplest necessities of life. My family had nothing, not food, not drink.

Date of Writing the Story: 2025/05/20

Noor Rafiq Rajeh

Age: 27 years

Original Place: Wadi Al-Arais

Place of Displacement: Al-Nufoukh Area

I lived with my husband and children in a small, modest house. My husband was ill and unable to work due to multiple health issues, and we struggled with poverty. Praise be to Allah for everything.

On the ominous day of October 7th, my family and I fled to Yafa in northern Gaza, then to a school, where I faced unbearable hardships: hunger, thirst, and extreme cold without blankets or warm clothes for my child. My heart burned with sorrow for him, yet I didn't know what to do.

Then we fled to Al-Zeitoun, to another school, where our suffering repeated itself due to ongoing problems and Israeli bombardments. There was no safe place left.

We were displaced many times, and with each displacement, our suffering intensified.

Now I live in a tent, unsure of what to do next. My family suffers from relentless hunger, thirst, and fear.

I pray that this nightmare ends soon. Praise be to Allah for everything, and Allah is sufficient for us, and He is the best protector.

Date of Writing the Story: 2025/05/18

Najla Mohammad Abu Ghaben

Age: 44 years

Original Place: Al-Shati Camp

Place of Displacement: Al-Rimal

I lived in a very modest house in Al-Shati Camp with my family. On October 7th, I fled to Deir Al-Balah, to the technical college, facing immense difficulties and tragedies at that moment.

After the ceasefire, I returned to Gaza, but the war resumed, bringing skyrocketing prices, deprivation, hunger, and fear. My children and I suffered from hunger, and I praise Allah for all circumstances.

I have a young daughter, and her father has abandoned her. I am raising my children alone. My mother is elderly, 80 years old, and sick, and I cannot face life's hardships alone. My situation is extremely difficult, what can I do? All I can do is pray.

O Allah, end this war, O Lord of the worlds.

Date of Writing the Story: 2025/05/21

Nibal Fathi Al-Sa'idi

Age: 18 years

Original Place: Al-Shati

Place of Displacement: The Sea

The war began on October 7th, and day by day, the situation worsened. Intense shelling struck every corner of Gaza. Leaflets ordering evacuation fell upon us, and we fled south on foot.

We suffered through the summer heat and freezing winter cold. Hunger became our reality as flour, food, drink, electricity, and safety were all denied to us. There was no safe place from the relentless Israeli bombardment.

We feared for our children, who were deprived of the simplest necessity in life, a loaf of bread. They cried day and night, searching for food to satisfy their hunger. Due to the lack of healthy food and water, diseases spread among children, ignorance grew, and darkness prevailed. Men were imprisoned and forced to return home disguised in women's clothing, while many of our relatives were martyred.

When we tried to buy canned goods, flour, sugar, or oil to feed the children, we couldn't afford them due to skyrocketing prices and our lack of money. Men were unemployed, and there were no clothes or blankets.

When we returned after the ceasefire, our homes were stolen and destroyed, leaving us with no shelter but tents. We lived in a tent by the sea, enduring the same suffering of hunger, oppression, and pain.

When will this war end? We want safety, freedom, and to live with dignity and peace. We want to live like the rest of the world, in peace and freedom. We seek mercy.

We, the children and women of Gaza, want freedom, safety, food, and to return to our normal lives.

Date of Writing the Story: 25/05/2025

Asma Imad Rajeh

Age: 35 years

Original Place: Al-Sha'af Area

Place of Displacement: Al-Sahaba Area

I lived with my family of six members. On October 7th, we fled our home due to missile attacks and went to Al-Zeitoun, taking nothing with us. I sought refuge at my parents' house and stayed there for several months, enduring numerous problems, the most significant being the lack of basic necessities like food. We suffered from hunger, thirst, and the absence of safety.

Then we fled south to Al-Nuseirat, where I had no clothes for my children or food. My husband, who was unemployed and ill, suffered from back and spinal pain. We endured severe cold, hunger, and thirst.

Each displacement brought more hunger, pain, and fear. When we returned to our homes, the war resumed, and we continued to suffer. Now we live in a tent instead of our home.

There is nothing left. My heart aches with unbearable pain. I hope this war ends soon.

Date of Writing the Story: 2025/05/03

Riham Rafiq Rajeh

Age: 25 years

Original Place: Al-Tuffah Area

Place of Displacement: Al-Nasr Area

On the ominous day of October 7th, our suffering began. On the first day, we fled to Al-Rimal, where we lived in a tent, enduring freezing cold, hunger, and fear. Then we were displaced again by the occupation from our land to the south. Due to the lack of food and water, we fled south to Deir Al-Balah, living in a tent.

We suffered from harsh winters and scorching summers, and my children's bodies were ravaged by insects like mosquitoes and hunger. Our greatest wish became obtaining a loaf of bread. Yes, holding a loaf of bread felt like holding a treasure. We craved everything.

Date of Writing the Story: 2025/05/07

Amena Ramy Rajeh

Age: 25 years

Original Place: Al-Zeitoun Area

Place of Displacement: Al-Tuffah Area

I was eagerly awaiting my wedding, which was just a week away, but my joy was cut short. On October 7th, our lives came to a halt. This war was unimaginable. I had been happy, but everything changed after October 7th. Celebrations turned into deep sorrow.

I married without a wedding ceremony and lived with my husband and his family in a tent. We suffered from hunger, fear, pain, and extreme cold. Then we fled to schools due to shelling and missiles. I was pregnant in my first month and sought refuge at my parents' house. I suffered from a lack of nutrition and clean water, and my husband was unemployed.

Thankfully, I gave birth to my son safely, but I couldn't celebrate like other mothers. We were in dire straits, and my son was deprived of basic necessities like milk and diapers. I was in agony, unsure of where to turn.

Thankfully, we returned to our homes, but found no houses, only tents, which became our companions in displacement. I hope this war ends soon, and our children can live like other children around the world.

Date of Writing the Story: 2025/04/24

Umm Diyaa Erheem

October 7, 2023... A date that cannot be forgotten, and a day unlike any other.

I am a mother of nine children, boys and girls. That morning, I began my day as usual, preparing breakfast for my children and getting them ready for school.

My little daughter stood in front of the mirror as I carefully arranged her hair, dressed her in her school uniform, and watched her hold her small backpack as if it carried her entire world between her hands.

Everything seemed ordinary until the first sound came.

The sound of rockets shook the walls, and my daughter's gaze shifted from the mirror to the window.

We rushed to the windows, unsure of what was happening...

In an instant, my morning turned into a nightmare.

A new war had begun, with the sounds of shelling everywhere.

That day... it was no ordinary day.

It was a day that stole peace from the hearts of mothers and turned the warmth of homes into ashes.

And so... the story began.

Yes, we thought it was just a story, a short tale that would pass quickly, ending within a day, a week, or even a month. We tried to reassure ourselves with words we didn't believe and convince our hearts that this wouldn't last long.

But unfortunately, it wasn't a story.

Destruction began, and fear grew day by day.

Every moment, the sound of explosions drew closer, and the expressions on my children's faces changed.

None of them asked anymore, "When will we go out?" or "When will we play"?

Instead, they started asking, "Mom, will we survive? Mom, will that plane take our house"?

I held them close, trying to protect them with my body, while inside, I was searching for someone to protect me from this terror.

The occupation intensified its attacks, drawing closer and closer to the homes: "There is no safe place here."

Each day became harder than the one before.

We lived under constant bombardment, slept to the sound of terror, and woke up to news of martyrs.

We could no longer endure.

We fled immediately, without much thought, taking only the souls we wanted to keep alive.

I left my home with my children, the home where we spent years of our lives, and left it behind.

We didn't look back because looking back meant death.

We headed to their grandmother's house, searching for safety in any corner, in any wall that hadn't yet collapsed.

We walked, carrying children, small bags, and hearts filled with fear.

Every step felt like crossing between life and death.

When we arrived, fear still clung to us.

We moved in silence, whispering as if loud voices might summon the shelling.

Even my children's laughter had disappeared.

After a long night of fear and terror, a night during which we didn't sleep, we decided to return home.

We told ourselves, "Praise be to Allah... the danger has passed."

We tried to convince our weary hearts that it was over, that everything had returned to normal.

But we didn't know what lay hidden in the moments ahead...

Not much time passed before the shelling returned, more intense, closer, and harsher.

We were forced to flee again.

This time, we went to my eldest daughter, who was married.

We crowded into her small house, trying to share security as we shared bread.

But the situation grew more dangerous.

The entire neighborhood came under attack, and the planes never left our skies.

So, we decided to leave once more in a new displacement, destination unknown, end uncertain.

We arrived at a school; the classroom was small, barely large enough to fit us.

No mattresses, no blankets, nothing but walls and the ground.

Yet… it gave us a small sense of safety.

Just a little, but it was enough to catch our breath.

Our only hope was that this would be the last displacement.

That we wouldn't have to flee again.

That we wouldn't carry our children at night, running amidst shrapnel and darkness.

Then… after a month spent in the school, on cold floors and under the sounds of shells,

They bombed the school's bathrooms. My hand and my son's hand were injured, but thank Allah, the injuries were minor.

Then came another displacement.

We were forced to leave the first school because the occupation forces were approaching.

Tanks could now be seen from distant windows,

And fear… always preceded us wherever we went.

We fled to a second school.

We thought it was safer, but war leaves no place untouched.

Then came the fourth displacement, the harshest of all.

More than fifty people crammed into one classroom.

No space to stretch our legs, no air, no privacy.

Men slept in the hallways, and women hugged their children in the corners.

There was no night we recognized, no day we rested in.

We heard whispers: "On the fourth day, a ceasefire will be announced."

We clung to it like a drowning person clings to a straw.

But just ten minutes before the ceasefire…

The school turned into hell.

Sudden shelling.

Martyrs.

Screams.

Prayers mixed with tears.

People ran under fire, trying to save themselves in any way possible.

We fled the school as the sky rained fire.

Then came the ceasefire… as if mocking us.

We returned to the school, its walls punctured, its roof cracked, and death still lurking in the corners.

We spent a week of "safety," but it wasn't true safety.

Then the war returned, as if it had never left.

The situation worsened.

There was no food, no water, no flour.

We looked at our children's faces, unsure of what to feed them.

Aid arrived, yes, but it wasn't enough.

People waited all day, from morning until evening, standing in lines just to get a bag of flour or a can of food to feed their children, who now fell asleep from hunger rather than exhaustion.

And then came the fifth displacement… they didn't stop.

We woke to terrifying sounds, got up quickly, packed our things,

And fled to another school.

We didn't know where to go, but we walked, I and my eldest son, who was married, and headed to relatives of my brother's wife.

They were stationed in a lab, and we slept on the stairs...

Four days without blankets, without anything.

My husband bought two sheets, and we covered ourselves with them, barely.

During those days, we ate flour mixed with sand, bread with sand, and tried to survive,

Because famine was growing and hurting more than anything else.

On the fourth day, they bombed the area around the school...

We escaped death once again, running to save our lives.

This time, we went to an institute called "Al-Amal" (Hope), gathering ourselves there.

We stayed in a small tent, covering ourselves after immense suffering that cannot be described.

We stayed at Al-Amal Institute for a short period, but it was among the hardest days...

Still, we did not lose hope. We found comfort in faith in Allah, waiting for relief we didn't know when would come.

Unfortunately, the war is still ongoing, and we don't know when or how it will stop.

Despite everything we've been through, I still stand every morning, arranging my daughter's hair, trying to reclaim a normal moment from a time that no longer exists.

I hug my children, feed them whatever is available, and hide my tears whenever they ask, "When will the war end"?

I mask my fear with words of reassurance and convince myself that tomorrow will be better.

Despite the exhaustion, displacement, loss, and hunger... I still give them love and the sense of security I lost.

That despite everything, we are still alive.

And that someday, we will tell this story while sitting in our homes, not in tents or schools.

We will recount it to our grandchildren… about patience we never knew we had and strength we never imagined we could endure.

Umm Kamil Abu Al-Kheir

Age: 45 years

Original Place: Al-Shuja'iyya

Place of Displacement: West Gaza

I am Umm Kamil, and I won't tell you my age, it suffices to say that I've lived and seen much. By Allah, this war made me witness misery, and I fled. How many times did I flee? Nearly twenty times or more, each time thinking this place was safe, only to find ourselves gathering our belongings and fleeing again.

I am a widow, may Allah have mercy on your father, Kamil. I raised my children as orphans, alone; and by Allah, no one understood my suffering except Him.

My children grew up, each going their own way, but thank Allah, they haven't forgotten me or abandoned me.

But alas, happiness didn't last. My eldest son, Kamil, my beloved and the light of my eyes, was martyred. He left and never returned. May Allah have mercy on him and grant him paradise. My heart broke, I can't describe how I felt. The whole world turned black in my eyes.

But Allah never forgets anyone. My children are my responsibility, I'm the one who raised and nurtured them. True, I'm older now, and true, I'm tired from displacement and sorrow, but when I look into their eyes, I remember Kamil and remind myself that I must be strong for them.

These are difficult days, Allah knows, very difficult days. But I remain patient, hoping for reward from Allah. I only wish for the war to end, for us to return to our homes, and live in peace and safety. I wish for Kamil's children to grow up and become better than me and their father. I wish to see them succeed and happy.

Allah is generous; He will not abandon us.

Date of Writing the Story: 2025/06/01

Yasmeen Nasser Helles

Age: 29 years

Original Place: Al-Shuja'iyya

I am Yasmeen Helles, twenty-nine years old, a widow. That word weighs on my heart like mountains, but it is my reality. My husband, may Allah have mercy on him, passed away in the West Bank in a horrific car accident. I became a widow in the prime of my youth, but life does not stop. I returned to Gaza, to the warmth of my family, to childhood memories that were a balm for my wounds.

But even Gaza, which I thought would be my final refuge, was not spared from the cruelty of fate. The war! A merciless war that shows no pity to the weak and knows no compassion. I fled with my family, leaving behind our home, our memories, and everything we owned. From Gaza to Rafah, then to Mawasi Deir Al-Balah, a small point on the map, but a world full of suffering.

Here, in this makeshift temporary camp, I live breathing fear. Fear of shelling, fear of losing more loved ones, fear of the unknown. The tents are cramped together, faces pale, and eyes tearful. We all wait, wait for a glimmer of hope, an end to this catastrophe.

But deep inside, there is a small spark igniting, a spark of the desire to live, a spark of hope for a better future. I watch the children playing with dirt, hear their faint laughter, and know that life will continue despite everything.

I will wait impatiently, tears held captive in my eyes. I will wait while clinging to hope, waiting while believing that tomorrow will be better. I wait for the crossings to open, I wait for life.

Date of Writing the Story: 2025/06/01

Mona Sami Abu Al-Kheir

Age: 35 years

Original Place: Al-Shuja'iyya

My name is Mona, and I am not just a name, I am the story of Palestine walking on two legs. I graduated in Islamic Studies, meaning I was supposed to be a teacher of generations, but life had something else in store for me.

In 2014, the war destroyed everything, homes, dreams, and even my health. The shelling led me to discover the wretched cancer that clung to me like roots cling to an olive tree. Since then, I've been caught in a whirlpool of chemotherapy, trying to live while carrying the weight of the world's pain inside me.

I thought 2014 was the worst thing that could happen, but it seems I was wrong. The recent war made me flee once, twice, three times. Each time, I gathered the scattered pieces of myself and a few simple belongings, fleeing to save my life.

When I thought it was over and returned to northern Gaza, a bit of hope lit up inside me. I thought perhaps Allah had written for me to live and bury my face in my land. But that hope didn't last long. Threats began to arrive, frightening words that made one tremble with fear. There was no solution but to flee again.

This time, there was no house to return to, no wall to lean my back against. I fled to a tent, a simple canvas tent, but inside it was my entire world. My medication, a few books, and most importantly… my Quran.

This Quran is not just a book; it is my companion, my friend, and my medicine. Whenever I feel the world closing in on me, I open the Quran and read. The verses fall upon my heart like cool water in the scorching heat. They give me strength and patience to carry on.

In the tent, amidst the cold and dust, I feel strong. Not because I am a superhero, no. It's because I hold onto Allah's words. His words are what sustain me, telling me that no matter how long the night, dawn will come.

Yes, I am sick, displaced, and have lost much, but I am still "Mona," who dreams of a free Palestine, who dreams of a day when I can teach my country's children the Quran and instill in them love for Allah and the land.

I still have breath in me, and I still have a Quran in my lap. That is enough to face any calamity and continue my journey, confident that Allah is with me.

Date of Writing the Story: 2025/06/02

Manar Mohammad Al-Dahdouh

Age: 26 years

Original Place: Al-Zeitoun Area

I am Manar. I live in the Al-Zeitoun neighborhood here in Gaza. Originally from Al-Shuja'iyya, I am the daughter of Al-Shuja'iyya's pride, but fate played its game. I got married and moved to Al-Zeitoun, and my family, Allah be with them, have been displaced since the start of the war, moving every day, staying everywhere in the south.

At that time, I was pregnant with my son Izzat, my eldest. Oh, how my heart aches, I was in my fourth month, and the world was pitch black. Hunger was unbearable; we couldn't find a clean bite to eat. Imagine, we started eating animal feed! May Allah be our witness. There was no food at all, and I was pregnant, meaning I needed two meals instead of one.

When it was time to give birth, oh, how alone I felt. My family was far away, in the south, while I was in Al-Zeitoun. I wished my mother was by my side, I wished my sister was here to hold my hand. I longed for someone from my family to be there, but the war had separated us. I gave birth to Izzat, thank Allah he was born safely, but my heart was broken. I couldn't see my family, couldn't show them my grandson. Five months passed, feeling like five years. The war raged on, the shelling never stopped, and fear settled in our hearts.

But praise be to Allah, He is great. After five months, there was a ceasefire. Oh, what joy! My family was able to return to the north, to devastated Al-Shuja'iyya. As soon as they returned, they came to see me in the Al-Zeitoun area. Oh, what an emotional moment! My mother hugged me and cried, and my father kissed my head. And when they saw Izzat, my grandson, oh, how cherished he was, they couldn't believe their eyes. Izzat was the light of our lives.

Oh Allah, may this war end, and may we return to living like human beings. Oh Allah, may Gaza return better than before, and may we reunite with our families and loved ones. And oh Allah, may no one endure what we have endured.

Date of Writing the Story: 2025/05/28

Subhiya Saleh Abu Samrah

Original Place: Wadi Al-Arais

My house was full of life, filled with the scent of my family and people. When the first catastrophe struck, I welcomed brothers and their father, my home became a warm embrace for everyone. Suddenly, oh, the sorrow in my heart, they dropped threatening leaflets and evacuation orders, as if throwing death upon us while we were wide awake.

We left our homes like those rising from graves, not knowing where to go or which way to turn. We went south, thinking it would be the lesser evil. But war is war, it doesn't distinguish between north and south. We were hungry, exhausted, and witnessed misery. What could we do? We said, "Praise be to Allah," perhaps He is testing our patience.

After a while, they told us to return to the north, saying the situation was safe. Oh, what short-lived joy! We returned to our destroyed homes, but at least we smelled the earth, the scent of home. We stayed there, like people waiting for death. We couldn't believe it when the war returned like a ravenous beast, devouring everything green and dry.

This time, we didn't know where to go. We sought refuge in a school, just like the poor people around us. The school, my son, was filled with weary faces, tearful eyes, and frightened children. We lost hope, my son. We lost hope in this life that refuses to smile upon us.

But what can we do? We continue to pray to Allah; He alone knows our condition. Perhaps Allah will have mercy on us and lift this dark cloud. Allah is generous, Allah is generous.

Date of Writing the Story: 2025/06/01

Sabah Al-Harazeen

Original Place: Al-Zeitoun

I remember everything as if it happened yesterday. Throughout the war, we never left our home, patience was our weapon. But when "Abd" – may Allah have mercy on him and heal every sick person – my precious son, fell severely ill, fear consumed my heart. He had cancer, Allah forbid it from your children, and the doctors said he needed to travel to Egypt for treatment.

We got him an exit permit, and we thanked Allah, seeing a glimmer of hope. Abd, may Allah have mercy on him, decided to flee so he could travel to Egypt. He didn't want to stay in the house and risk his health, it meant everything to him.

As soon as he arrived at Al-Shifa Hospital, tears filled my eyes when he saw his siblings! They were displaced in the south, fleeing bombardment and death, but death pursued them wherever they went. Oh, how my heart ached for them, and in that moment, Abd passed away. We decided to flee south to bid him farewell and bury him. May Allah grant us patience and strength in this world.

Date of Writing the Story: 2025/06/01

Manal Mohammad Abu Al-Kheir

Age: 50 years

Original Place: Al-Shuja'iyya

Oh, how cruel this world is! My name is Manal Abu Al-Kheir, mother of six children, may Allah protect them. I was born in Kuwait, but fate brought me to Gaza. I got married and settled here, while my parents, may Allah have mercy on them, stayed in Kuwait. All my life has been in Gaza; I love it and its people, but this war has broken my back. Allah forbid anyone from seeing what we've witnessed. Displacement has become part of our lives, moving from house to house, from area to area, searching for safety.

During this cursed war, Allah blessed my daughter with her first child, my first grandchild. Oh, what joy that was short-lived! I wasn't with her during childbirth, I didn't see her bring him into the world! My heart ached, wishing I could be there to ease her pain and pray to Allah to ease her delivery.

But praise be to Allah. When things calmed down a little and we returned north, the first thing I did was go see my grandson. Oh, my soul adores him, a small angel, sleeping peacefully as if the world isn't falling apart. I held him in my arms, and tears fell uncontrollably. Tears of joy and pain, tears of fear and hope.

I said to myself, "O Allah, this new generation, this is the hope that remains. O Allah, protect him, protect our children, and all the people of Gaza."

I know these days are tough, and we still have a long road ahead, but when I saw my grandson, I felt a new strength, a strength that helps me endure and keep going, for my children, for my grandchildren, so that Gaza remains steadfast. May Allah be with us.

Date of Writing the Story: 2025/06/01

Umm Omar Helles

Original Place: Al-Shuja'iyya

I am Umm Omar Helles. By Allah, I've lived long enough to see life in its sweetness and bitterness. Wars and calamities have passed over me, Allah forbid they return, but this war... it's unlike anything else. You feel like a wounded bird, flapping your wings but not knowing where to go.

The house in the north was my whole life, it held the memories of my children and grandchildren. But what can we do? The order came to evacuate, and we left everything behind. We fled once, twice, three times, each time packing our belongings onto a cart and walking, not knowing where to find refuge.

We thought, "Thank Allah, the war is over, and we're back home in the north." Oh, how I wish we hadn't returned! The house was still standing, but where was the safety? It was gone. They told us again to leave, calling it a "danger zone." Well, where should we go? Where can we escape death?

All we found was a tent. A worn-out tent, battered by the sun and wind from every direction. But praise be to Allah for His covering. I gathered my children and grandchildren around me, each of us burdened with worry and fear.

What can we do, my dear? This is life, sometimes it's good, sometimes it's bad. We endure, and we pray to Allah to relieve us. The important thing is to stay united and protect our children from fear.

You know, my dear, at night when my grandchildren are asleep, I look up at the sky. I see the stars twinkling and say to myself, "O Allah, just as this sky is vast, Your relief is even vaster. Do not forget us, O Allah."

And Allah willing, He will not forget us, and He will grant us victory over oppression. There will come a day when we return to our homes and plant roses and jasmine there. But we need patience and prayer. Allah is generous, my dear, Allah is generous.

Date of Writing the Story: 2025/06/01

Amal Helles

Age: 20 years

Original Place: Al-Shuja'iyya

I am Amal Helles, twenty years old. If only time could stop when one is happy, but alas, life often goes against our wishes. You see, I'm a newlywed bride, I had been married for just two weeks when this war suddenly struck us.

I remember that day as if it were yesterday. Life was normal, and then suddenly, we heard the sound of shelling. Oh Allah, our hearts dropped to our feet. We didn't know what to do, everyone was screaming and running. There was no time to think. Instinctively, we decided to head south, like everyone else. We left our home, left all our belongings, my dowry that I hadn't even had time to enjoy, all of it left behind. We thought it would be just a few days before we returned, but the ordeal turned out to be much longer than that.

In the south, we endured days that Allah forbid anyone from experiencing. We stayed in a school with a hundred other families, all crammed together. Food was scarce, water was limited, and the conditions in the bathroom were unbearable. But praise be to Allah for everything, what matters most is that we were alive.

Allah blessed me with pregnancy. I was overjoyed beyond measure, thinking it was Allah's compensation. And indeed, I gave birth to my firstborn son, Omar. How can I describe my joy with him? He was my whole world, my hope. But oh, what fleeting joy it was!

We couldn't keep Omar safe. After a few months, they ordered us to evacuate our homes once again.

Now here I am, sitting in a tent, holding Omar close and afraid for his safety. I don't know what fate holds for us, but what I do know is that Allah is great, and He will surely relieve us. What can we do? This is life, sometimes it's good, sometimes it's bad.

Date of Writing the Story: 2025/05/28

Ghadeer Al-Harazeen

Age: 27 years

Original Place: Al-Zeitoun

If only the world would show us a little mercy. I am Ghadeer, like any woman in Gaza; my life was going along with blessings, a simple job, family gatherings, and the laughter of my daughter Maram, which meant the world to me. But suddenly, everything turned upside down.

When the war began, we didn't think much about it, like everyone else, we packed our things and fled to the south. We left our home, memories, and everything behind, hoping to find a safe place to stay. We spent days in a tent, enduring cold, heat, and illness. Little Maram couldn't handle it; every other day, we rushed her to the nearest medical center.

We returned to the north. True, the house was damaged, but we said, "Praise be to Allah." We stayed for about forty days, trying to restore our daily routine. Maram started laughing and playing again, and I felt hope returning.

But alas, joy never lasts. Suddenly, the evacuation order came. Where should we go now? We're exhausted, truly exhausted. We don't know how to live or even how to die. My husband sat overwhelmed, not knowing what to do or where to take us. I held Maram's hand and started reciting Quran for her, hoping Allah would guide us.

We don't know what fate holds for us, but what we do know is that the people of Gaza have not surrendered, and they never will. We remain steadfast, continue praying, and hold onto our land and dignity. May Allah support each and every one of us.

Date of Writing the Story: 2025/06/01

Hadeel Ayyad

Age: 30 years

My name is Hadeel, married with two beautiful children, Jilan and Jameel. From the start of the war, we were forced to leave our home in Gaza and flee to the south. Those were difficult days, fear and terror beyond description, but we kept saying, "Praise be to Allah that we are still alive."

When they announced that returning to the north was allowed, we thought it was over, that the nightmare was nearly over. We decided to return to our home, no matter its condition, it would be better than displacement and humiliation. We returned, our hearts pounding, afraid of what we might find.

Oh, how I wish we hadn't returned! When we arrived, we found the house destroyed, collapsed to the ground. Not a single stone remained standing on another. The world turned black before my eyes. Where should we go? Where should we live?

We had no choice but to search for any place to shelter us. We found a school that opened its doors to displaced families. We set up a small tent inside the schoolyard and said, "Praise be to Allah," grateful for a roof to protect us from the sun and rain.

But happiness never lasts. Barely two days passed when the situation worsened, the shelling intensified, and we barely had time to settle into the tent before we were forced to leave it and flee again.

And here I am now, displaced for the thousandth time, not knowing where to go or where to settle. But our hope in Allah remains strong, and we pray that He will relieve us and all the people of Gaza. May Allah give us patience and strength.

Date of Writing the Story: 2025/06/01

Story (101)

Bana Mohammad Abu Al-Kheir

Age: 15 years

Original Place: Al-Zeitoun Area

I was in ninth grade before the war came and destroyed everything. We used to dream of school, new backpacks, and laughing with our friends, but suddenly everything changed.

That day, the sound of planes shook the earth, and fear settled in our hearts. Houses were demolished, streets were destroyed, and everyone fled. We left everything behind and ran, searching for any safe place to sleep.

We reached a camp for displaced people, a cluster of tents side by side. It was scorching during the day and freezing at night. Though the situation was difficult, my mother, Allah bless her, always told us, "Education is your weapon, girls. Don't let the war steal your future." And indeed, amidst the tents, sorrow, and pain, they opened a small tent they called the "Hope Educational Tent." It consisted of a small board, a few books, and a teacher trying to make up for the school we lost.

On the first day, I went to the tent feeling scared and hesitant. But when I saw my friends, the same faces I used to see at school, I felt a small spark of joy. The teacher was very kind, trying to explain lessons to us and encourage us.

It wasn't like school; there were no books or comfortable chairs, but we tried to learn whatever we could, drawing, writing, reading stories, and dreaming of returning to our schools and homes as they once were.

The war destroyed many things, but it couldn't steal our dreams. We still dream, learn, and pray to Allah to bring peace back to Gaza so we can rebuild our future. That educational tent became like a glimmer of hope we clung to.

Date of Writing the Story: 2025/06/01

Lina Mohammad Abu Al-Kheir

Age: 25 years

Original Place: Al-Shuja'iyya

I am an intern doctor, still learning, but this learning came in the middle of war. My final year of medical school was a dream, almost within reach, but fate had other plans. Displacement scattered us from house to house, from tent to tent. This meant enduring cold and fear, yet I managed to complete my academic year and graduate. I received my diploma while sitting in displacement.

Now I work at a hospital, stories that would make your hair stand on end. Every day, I witness pain and despair. I see people losing their loved ones, and others giving birth amidst fear. I see children playing in the sand instead of swings, and youth dreaming of a future that seems shapeless.

Once, an elderly woman came to us searching for her son, missing for several days. We searched and asked around until we found him in the morgue. Oh Allah, it was such a difficult moment. How could I tell her that her son was gone? How could I console her?

Another time, a pregnant woman came in, suffering intense labor pains. The conditions were dire, lacking sufficient medicine and equipment. But thank Allah, He protected her, and she gave birth to her daughter safely. When I heard the baby's cry, I felt that there was still hope, and life persisted.

Each of these stories teaches me something new. They teach me patience, strength, and that medicine is not just about treatment, it's also about compassion and humanity. Yes, the situation is tough, and yes, the war has taken so much from us, but we, the people of Gaza, do not break. We remain steadfast, face challenges, and continue to dream of a better tomorrow.

Date of Writing the Story: 2025/06/01

Anwar Mohammad Abu Al-Kheir

Age: 20 years

Original Place: Al-Shuja'iyya

Just a week before the war began, I was over the moon with excitement. It was my first week at university! Oh, how thrilled I was. New clothes, new books, new friends... an indescribable feeling! I felt like I was opening a new chapter in my life, a chapter full of hope and dreams for the future.

But alas, happiness didn't last long. The war destroyed everything. Suddenly, our world turned upside down. The sound of shelling, fear in my family's eyes, neighbors running in the streets... Allah forbid those days from ever returning.

We were displaced many times, from house to house, from camp to camp. Each time, we'd pack our belongings, thinking, "Allah willing, this is the last time." But alas, every time, we ended up fleeing again.

The university? Gone were the dreams. Lectures moved to phones, and professors appeared on small screens. The internet was weak, electricity kept cutting off... torment beyond measure. But I told myself, I must endure. I must keep going.

I completed my first university year online, after immense struggle known only to Allah. But praise be to Him, I passed. I made my family proud. Despite everything, I proved to myself that I am strong.

The road ahead is still long, and there are many challenges. But I am optimistic. I know that Allah never forgets anyone. And Allah willing, after this darkness, our lives will return better than before. I will go back to university, study hard, and achieve all my dreams. And Allah willing, that's exactly what will happen.

Date of Writing the Story: 2025/06/01

Umm Shareef Abu Al-Kheir

Age: 54 years

Original Place: Al-Shuja'iyya

My life journey has not been easy, but what I endured during the war surpassed all hardships. My name is Umm Shareef, and I am the woman everyone knows in our neighborhood in Gaza. My life story is filled with pain and patience, especially my story with my son Shareef, who was my first joy and most precious possession.

Shareef was my eldest and firstborn son, the heart and soul of our home. But he was taken by the war. May Allah have mercy on him and grant him paradise. I remember the day he left, shelling was everywhere, and the world seemed engulfed in flames. Everyone was afraid and terrified, not knowing where to go or find refuge.

I decided to flee south with my daughters to stay with relatives. It was cramped, but thank Allah, they welcomed us with kindness. As for Shareef and his father, my husband, they refused to leave our home in the north. They said, "We must stay and protect our land. We won't let anyone take it from us."

Days passed, and the shelling continued. The sound of explosions shook the house, and my heart was always with them. Then one day, devastating news reached me, Shareef and his father had been arrested! The world turned black before my eyes; I felt as if my soul had left my body.

I prayed and cried every day, asking about them, but no one had answers. Days dragged on, and nights were long as I tried to bear it all. Despite this immense pain, I remained patient because life doesn't stop, and hope persists even when the heart feels crushed.

After some time, my husband returned to us. Joy returned, though my heart still ached for Shareef, who remains absent. I tried to stay strong for my children and daughters, reminding them that we must endure and hold onto life despite everything.

The war brought losses that can never be forgotten and deprived us of so much, but our determination remains unbroken. No words can describe the pain of a mother who lost her son, but deep inside, faith and patience sustain her, for patience is the key to relief.

I am Umm Shareef, amidst the rubble and tears. All I want is to live for my children, to see them safe and sound, whether the world stands with us or against us.

Date of Writing the Story: 2025/05/28

Umm Mohammad Mahdi

Age: 55 years

I am Umm Mohammad, like any mother in Gaza, with a heart full of pain. My married daughters fled south when things became unbearable in the north, we prioritized safety. Abu Mohammad and I stayed in our home; we couldn't leave it behind. Mahmoud, may Allah have mercy on him, always reassured us, saying, "Don't be afraid, Mother, I'm here."

But fate is merciless. One day, we heard a loud explosion nearby. Mahmoud was outside, and when he returned, his face was pale. He didn't say anything, but I knew something terrible had happened. Soon after, news of his martyrdom reached us. Oh, how I wished death had taken me before him; oh, how I wished!

My heart shattered, truly shattered. The world turned black before my eyes. Abu Mohammad couldn't bear it, he became silent, though his eyes told a story of immense sorrow.

Later, during the ceasefire, my daughters returned from the south. Oh, how happy I was to see them! I hugged them and cried, cried for Mahmoud, cried for our situation, and cried for all of Gaza. They saw me broken, but their presence gave me some strength.

My daughters began helping me, easing the burden for me and their father. My eldest daughter said, "Mother, Mahmoud is gone, but his spirit is still with us. We must be strong for him." Her words comforted me a little; I felt there was still hope.

Life is hard, but we, the people of Gaza, have learned to endure and persevere. Though my heart aches for Mahmoud, my daughters and grandchildren are my support and pride. And Allah willing, He will help us rebuild Gaza, making it even better than before. May Allah give patience to every mother who lost her child in this war.

Date of Writing the Story: 2025/05/28

Maha Naeem Abdullah Qanoua

Original Place: Al-Shuja'iyya

This war has battered us in ways unimaginable. We've been displaced from one place to another, every time we think we've finally settled, we find ourselves having to pack up and move again.

Our home is gone, and sweet memories have turned into heartache. Life in tents is a different story altogether, no food like others have, no clean water to drink. Hunger has taken away our strength; we walk two steps and collapse from exhaustion and low blood sugar. Our energy is depleted, none of us can do anything anymore.

Winter was torture. The tent would flood, and the cold cut through our bones. Where could we go? To whom could we complain? The whole world seemed to turn its back on us.

And the worst part was the humiliation we faced, from those closest to us. This war showed us who truly cares and who doesn't. Some people helped us wholeheartedly, while others wouldn't lift a finger even if they saw us dying. It revealed people's true nature.

We're exhausted, so very tired. But what can we do? Our hope in Allah remains strong. I long to see peace return to our land, for us to go back to how things were, to our homes, to our lives. Allah is generous.

Date of Writing the Story: 2025/05/28

Umm Ahmad Tabash

Original Place: KhanYounis

I am Umm Ahmad Tabash, just like any other hardworking woman in Gaza, but Allah tested me with two sons who have autism and intellectual disabilities. May He heal them and grant them wellness, O Allah. I have five children, thank Allah for them, but taking care of these two boys comes with double the responsibility.

You know how Gaza is, always moving from one calamity to another. This last war, may Allah never bring it upon us again, devastated us beyond measure. Like everyone else, we fled our home, leaving everything behind as we ran for our lives. Oh, how I wish death had taken us instead of witnessing such humiliation.

The biggest challenge was with my sons. Do you know what it means to have a child with autism and intellectual disabilities living in a tent? Madness! The tent is cramped, the heat unbearable, people coming and going constantly, and the noise overwhelming. My boys couldn't handle the commotion or the crowds. They'd start screaming and acting out, and I didn't know what to do with them. If only someone could talk to them and understand them, but how can you explain things to someone who doesn't comprehend the world?

We moved from place to place, from a UNRWA school to a tent by the sea. Each location worse than the last. Wherever we went, we found the same suffering. Everyone was struggling and burdened, and who would bear the weight of my sons? Sometimes, I felt like a burden on others. I wished I hadn't given birth to them! But I seek forgiveness from Allah, they are my children, a part of me.

The hardest moments were when they fell ill. Can you imagine searching for medicine as though looking for treasure? Hospitals were overwhelmed, and doctors couldn't keep up. And then, how could I maintain their hygiene in the tent? Water was scarce, and soap nonexistent. I washed them with salty water, but what good does that do?

Sometimes, at night, I'd sit alone, look up at the sky, and pray to Allah. "O Allah," I'd say, "I know You test those You love, but please ease my burdens and those of my children. I'm not asking for wealth or luxury, I just want protection, health, and for my children to grow up safely."

Allah is merciful. We must remain patient and steadfast. We continue to pray that He eases our troubles and those of all the people of Gaza. May Allah help every mother with a sick child, and may He heal every patient soul. Such is life, one day belongs to you, and the next against you.

Date of Writing the Story: 2025/06/01

Umm Tareq Mahdi

Original Place: Sheikh Ajlin

I am Umm Tareq, known to everyone in the neighborhood. I have Tareq and several other children, boys and girls, may Allah protect them and keep them safe. And oh, my grandchildren, they filled my home with laughter and play. We lived modestly, content with what we had, grateful for His blessings. Tareq's father worked hard, and my mother helped me around the house and with the grandchildren.

But alas, the war came and took everything with it. I remember that day vividly, we were sitting, drinking morning tea, when suddenly we heard the sound of shelling nearby. The world turned into flames and smoke. Mohammad, Allah rest his soul, had gone out to buy bread. He never made it back.

Oh, the pain that struck my heart when I heard the news! The world turned black before my eyes. My son was gone, my pillar, a piece of my soul, taken away. How could anything replace his laughter, his words, his warm embrace that once comforted me? After that, life became harder and harder.

Our home was destroyed, and we started living in a tent, just like everyone else. The cold at night gnawed at our bones, and the scorching sun during the day burned us alive. Food was scarce, and water even scarcer. But what could we do? We said, "Praise be to Allah in every situation."

Tareq and his family tried to support me, but their situation wasn't much better than mine. Each of us carried the worries of the other. But the greatest tragedy remains the loss of Mohammad. Every time I see one of his grandchildren playing, I remember him, and my heart breaks anew.

Life is harsh, my child, but we must endure and persevere. Allah is kind, and Allah willing, He will relieve our suffering. We await the day we can return to our homes and live as we once did. And how I wish Mohammad could be with us, but may Allah have mercy on him and grant him the highest paradise.

Date of Writing the Story: 2025/05/28

Aisha

Age: 26 years

Original Place: Beit Lahia

I am Aisha, a nurse skilled in my work, but circumstances played their cruel game. I'm married with two children as beautiful as the moon, they were my entire life, filled with laughter and play. Before the war, life was going smoothly; work, home, and my kids were all fine. But suddenly, everything changed.

The war destroyed everything around us, houses were gone, and life became unbearably expensive. I sat pondering how to handle it all, how to feed my children and protect them from this situation.

I thought to myself, "Aisha, you're on your own." So I rented a small oven in the Al-Rimal area, just enough to get by, and started baking for people. Arabic bread, taboon bread, za'atar manakeesh, whatever they asked for. I woke up early every morning to knead and bake.

Working with the oven wasn't easy, heat, fire, and smoke surrounded me. But when I saw the sparkle in my children's eyes as they ate a clean meal, all the effort felt worth it. The neighbors began supporting me, buying from me, and praying for me. "Allah give you health, Aisha," they'd say, "and bless you with your children." Those prayers strengthened me and gave me hope.

Yes, I've grown tired, and yes, the war has shown me the harsh face of life. But it has also taught me to be strong, to rely on myself, and most importantly, not to lose hope in tomorrow. One day, my children will grow up, study, and support one another. And one day, Palestine will return better than before, and we'll laugh wholeheartedly like we used to.

Date of Writing the Story: 2025/05/28

Inas Bakroun

Age: 34 years

Original Place: Gaza

My name is Inas, from Gaza, my beloved. I married young, but Allah didn't grant me a lasting share; I divorced and had a daughter as beautiful as the moon, named Hala. After some time, Allah blessed me again, and I remarried. Praise be to Him, we settled into a stable life.

But alas, this cursed war came along. The world turned upside down. Houses were destroyed, people were martyred, and fear took root in our hearts day and night. We decided to flee from death, displaced like so many others, searching for a safe place to take refuge.

During our displacement, Israeli forces struck a UNRWA school where we thought we'd find safety. Oh, what my eyes witnessed! My husband was hit in the leg, may Allah have mercy on him. The doctors tried to save him, but it was no use, his soul returned to its Creator. I became a widow once again, and my daughter Hala an orphan. Yet the war continued, and death lingered all around us. Praise be to Allah for everything; He never forgets His servants. Now, I care for Hala and her siblings, trying to provide them with everything they need. I am both mother and father now, praying to Allah to give me strength and guidance.

May Allah grant us patience and strength, and relieve us and all the people of Gaza. I long for the return of happy days, to see my daughter grow, learn, and live in safety. I dream of seeing Gaza smile again.

Date of Writing the Story: 2025/05/28

Suhaila Bakroun

Age: 36 years

Original Place: Al-Shuja'iyya

The war shattered us and forced us from our homes. We had been living peacefully, barely making ends meet, but praise be to Allah, we were managing. Suddenly, the world turned upside down.

I remember that night, we were sitting down to dinner, just finishing up, when we heard an explosion that shook the house to its core. My children were terrified and started crying, and my heart sank into my chest. My husband, may Allah heal him, went to check what was happening, and he returned bleeding heavily. His injury was severe, and he couldn't move.

We quickly gathered what little we could, a few clothes, and fled. We left everything behind: our home, memories, and dreams. We walked for days and nights, not knowing where we were headed, our only goal was to escape death.

We arrived at a UNRWA school, where people like us, displaced and frightened, had taken shelter. The conditions were dire: no food, no clean water, and nowhere decent to sleep. But praise be to Allah, people helped one another. We shared bread and drops of water, praying for relief.

My husband is still unwell, and we can't find proper treatment for him. Medicine is scarce, and doctors are overwhelmed. But I refuse to give up. I gather my strength for the sake of my children and my husband. I must be strong to protect and support them.

Every day, I pray to Allah to bring us back to our homes, to let us live in peace and security. I long for my children to laugh and play like they used to. I wish to see my husband healthy again. I dream of the war ending so we can rebuild our lives anew.

We await relief from Allah, praying for peace to descend upon us. Oh Allah, spare others from witnessing what we have seen.

Date of Writing the Story: 2025/05/28

Manal Esdodi

Age: 26 years

Original Place: Al-Shuja'iyya

Oh Allah, life is so bleak and chaotic, no one knows where to turn. I'm Manal, living in Gaza, married with two daughters as beautiful as the moon. Life was going well, thank Allah, but suddenly everything turned upside down.

When the war began, we didn't know where to go. Fear gripped our hearts, and the sound of shelling kept us awake at night. We thought Shahed a Al-Aqsa Hospital might be the safest place, so my husband, daughters, and I went there and stayed for a few days. It was chaos, everyone scared and sick, but at least we were together. When things seemed to calm down a bit, we decided to look for another place. A tent seemed better, at least being outside felt safer than staying in the hospital. We moved to an area with tents and stayed there for a while. Those were tough days: scorching heat during the day, freezing cold at night, little food or water, but we tried to stay patient and prayed for relief.

After some time, we heard that conditions in the north had improved. We decided to return to check on our homes and land. But oh, how I wish we hadn't gone back! The houses were destroyed, streets covered in rubble, but we thanked Allah we were alive. We stayed for a few days trying to clean and fix the house, but we never got to enjoy it.

Suddenly, they announced another evacuation order! Oh Allah, what kind of life is this? We barely returned home, and now we're being forced to leave again. We didn't know where to go, the fear returned to our hearts. We quickly grabbed a few belongings and fled once more.

Now I sit here in the tent, unsure of what will happen next. Everything feels like a fog, but our hope in Allah remains strong. We pray He relieves us and all the people of Gaza, returning each of us safely to our homes. Allah is generous.

Date of Writing the Story: 2025/05/28

Samira Qreqea

Original Place: Wadi Al-Arais

Displacement is humiliation, there's no dignity left. Every day, you're thrown into the dirt, searching for crumbs to survive. But me? I don't like to beg. All my life, I've held my head high, a trait I inherited from my late mother, may Allah have mercy on her.

When we settled into this tattered tent, I told myself, "Ya Umm Hassan, this isn't how we live. You need to find work, something to preserve your dignity." The first thing that came to mind was building a clay oven, an old skill passed down from my family.

I gathered some bricks and mud, and built a small oven, just big enough for two or three loaves of bread. At first, I worried people wouldn't trust me, but praise be to Allah, my reputation preceded me. Everyone knows Umm Hassan is clean, and her work is spotless.

I started baking for people. Sure, the money is little, but it's better than nothing. Imagine this: someone comes to me with just enough flour for two loaves, and I bake them with all my heart. I'd never cheat or steal even a grain of flour. Allah blesses honest work.

Life is hard, I won't lie to you. Water is scarce, firewood is expensive, and flour has become as precious as gold. But what can we do? We live and try. Every time I light the oven, I pray to Allah to relieve us, to bring us back safely to our homes. And I tell myself, "Ya Umm Hassan, as long as the oven is lit, there's hope."

Date of Writing the Story: 2025/06/01

Aseel Rizq Abu Al-Kheir

Age: 17 years

Original Place: Al-Shuja'iyya

My name is Aseel, and I'm in my final year of high school. Right now, I should be studying and reviewing for exams, but where is there room for that? The world is on fire, filled with shelling and missiles. You don't know where to turn, to escape the fear or the worry about a future that seems shapeless.

Every day, we wake up to the sound of shelling, praying that the day passes without harm, that we don't lose anyone close to us. Studying? Who has the heart to open a book? Still, deep inside, there's a small spark of hope, a candle lighting the darkness. Hope that the war will end soon, that we'll return to normal life and be able to take our exams like everyone else.

I remember when we were in school, dreaming about university. Each of us had plans, what we wanted to study, what we wanted to become. I want to study architecture, to build new homes to replace the ones that were destroyed.

Right now, all we wish for is to stay alive, to see our families and friends safe. But still, we haven't forgotten the dream of university. We pray to Allah to relieve us, to let us achieve our dreams and make up for all the lost time.

Oh Allah, You know our condition, You see what's happening to us. Oh Allah, Your relief is near, and Your victory is coming.

Date of Writing the Story: 2025/06/01

Iman

Age: 40 years

Original Place: An-Nuseirat

I am Iman, a mother of five children, may Allah protect them and grant them long lives. All my life, I've loved life and cherished simple joys. But since the war began, we've been displaced repeatedly, like migrating birds with nowhere to rest. Every time, we carry a few belongings and flee from places we thought were safe, but there's no real safety here.

We left our homes and memories behind, our hearts heavy with pain. I saw my children crying because they left their rooms, their toys, their animals, everything they cherished. I tried to comfort them: "Don't be afraid, my darlings. Allah is generous; we'll find a better place and tell our stories again." But even I was scared, scared of the unknown, of the future, of the relentless shelling.

The nights were cold, and we slept in schools, in tents, sometimes on the ground. Food was scarce, the cold harsh, and our hearts constantly fearful of planes and bombs. The children grew weary, and my eyes never stopped crying for them. Every day, I prayed to Allah to ease their suffering, but life wasn't easy.

I tried to strengthen my children, telling them stories of patience, strength, and hope. I'd always say, "Tomorrow will be better, my children. The sun will rise for us." Those words gave me strength too.

After months of hardship, we heard news that we might return north, to our homes. What joy! My spirit returned, and my children ran around me, saying, "Mom, we're going back to our house, to our rooms, to our toys!" They were happy, their hearts full of hope.

When we returned, my heart broke. Many houses were destroyed, streets ruined, and life's thorns blocked our path. But our house was still standing. Praise Allah. It stood despite everything, as if saying, "I'm here; I didn't leave you alone."

I opened the door, and the familiar scent of our old home reached me, the smell of memories. Dust covered everything, but for the first time in a long while, I felt safe. My children ran around, exploring every corner, their rooms, their toys, even the chair they loved.

The road ahead is long and difficult, and we'll need to work hard to restore everything. But the most important thing is that we're back home, in our space, feeling a sense of peace.

Every day, I pray to Allah to compensate us with good, to give us the strength to endure and build a new life, a life full of hope and joy, free from fear and pain. The war took much from us, but it didn't take our will, because our strength lies in being together.

I am Iman, a patient mother, with a big heart and a spirit that doesn't break. My family, my children, are the ones who give me life, the light in my eyes amidst all this darkness.

Date of Writing the Story: 2025/06/01

Umm Na'eem Naser

Age: 55 years

Original Place: Rafah

I am the mother of two precious hearts: Maram, my daughter, a fifth-year medical student, and Hasan, my eldest son, who has autism. I pray he completes his journey and achieves his dreams, and I ask Allah for the patience to care for him.

When they told us we had to leave our home in Rafah, my heart shattered. We knew it wouldn't be easy, but we had no choice. We left the house where we'd lived for years, leaving behind a lifetime of memories, and fled without hope or safety.

With Hasan, the situation was even harder. He can't speak or hear well, and adapting to these constant changes is difficult for him. In every place we went, he either sat quietly or became anxious. I tried to understand him and support him, but how? No one understands his condition except us, and no one helps us in these harsh conditions of displacement.

My husband, though weak, sacrificed himself for us, but the burden grew heavy on him. I was the only one trying to handle everything. There was no one, no young neighbor or relative, to stand by us. We were lost and broken between displacement, cold, and hunger.

We slept in schools, in cramped tents, sometimes without electricity or warmth, our hearts always fearful for Hasan, worried his condition would worsen. Despite her struggles, Maram tried to keep us hopeful.

The days of displacement were long, each day the same struggle. We prayed for patience and relief, longing to return to the homes we were forced to leave. But until today, we haven't returned. Every time I think of Hasan and his autism, my heart aches beyond words.

As I sit here telling you my story, I wait for the crossing to open. My true companion here is patience, waiting for a chance to leave with Maram, Hasan, and my family to seek refuge in Libya, hoping for safety and a new beginning. I miss fresh air, peace, and a better life for my children, especially Hasan, whose life depends on our stability and protection.

The crossing is often closed, and the waiting kills the soul, but I cling to hope. I tell myself, Allah willing, He will open the crossing for us, and we'll find a place that protects and shelters my children, especially Hasan, whose condition requires care we can't find here.

I am a mother who endures, who fights, waiting for relief so I can give my children the life they deserve, far from the sound of shelling, far from the pain of displacement, far from the fear that never leaves us.

Date of Writing the Story: 2025/06/01

Lina

Age: 36 years

Original Place: KhanYounis

I am Lina, cheerful and love to breathe fresh air and live in the moment. But war after war, Allah help us. When they said "displacement," my heart sank. How could we leave our home and all of Gaza? But what could we do? Fear overpowered us. We packed a few belongings, as much as we could, me and my children, and headed to Rafah.

Rafah was like a boiling pot, people on top of people, tents crammed together. Oh Allah, how do people live like this? Heat, salty water, and the kids always needing something. We stayed like that for a few weeks, waiting for relief. But I don't like despair, I encouraged the kids every day: "Tomorrow will be better, tomorrow we'll return home."

And truly, Allah never forgets His servants. When things started calming down a bit, I told the kids: "Come on, let's go back home. Sure, it might be a little damaged, but it's still our home, with the scent of Gaza in it." We returned, oh Allah, what joy it was! The house needed some work and cleaning, but the important thing was that we were back. As soon as I entered, I smelled the scent of the house, the scent of memories. I hugged the walls and said, "I missed you, my home."

The kids were happy too, each running to their room to check it out. We started cleaning and organizing, and little by little, the house began to shine again like before. True, fear is still there, and the shelling hasn't stopped completely, but hope is also present. We try to bring life back to how it was, to laugh, play, and eat good food. Life requires a bit of patience and strength, and we, the people of Gaza, are capable of that.

One day, as I was sitting in front of the house sweeping dust and preparing some tea over the fire, my neighbor Umm Mohammad came over. She looked exhausted and broken. She told me their house had been completely destroyed, and they were still living in tents. I told her: "Umm Mohammad, come sit, this is your home just as it is mine."

She came in, her eyes filled with tears but smiling. We sat and drank tea together while she told me about the old days, how her kids grew up in this house, and how the war scattered us. We talked, laughed, and cried, it was as if we were bringing life back to the neighborhood.

My kids brought some bread and thyme, and we sat eating together on the floor, just like we always did before the war. At that moment, I felt the house had become a home again, not just four walls.

Warmth doesn't come from the walls, it comes from people, from gatherings, from neighbors, from kindness that doesn't die despite all the suffering.

From that day on, whenever I hear about someone returning or lost, I open my door and say: "There's a place here, even if small, but with a big heart."

And every day, I teach my kids that despite the pain, the people of Gaza always return to sow joy, even among the rubble.

Date of Writing the Story: 2025/06/01

Maram Salem Saad

Age: 18 years

Original Place: Al-Shuja'iyya

My name is Maram, a Tawjihi student, and I had planned to get a high grade and leave Gaza. My dream was to study medicine abroad, but this war changed everything.

I studied day and night, hard and with passion, treating every book as a ticket to travel. I imagined myself at university, wearing the white coat, helping people. But suddenly, everything stopped.

Our home became deserted, books turned into memories, and studying became a luxury, not a right. We wait, we wait for the war to end, for some good news, for our stolen lives to return.

Every day passes, and I wish to open my books again, to dream again, to plan again. But at the same time, I try to stay strong, help my family, and remain optimistic.

Hope is still alive, and I still dream of the day I take my exams, achieve my dreams, and make my family proud. I still dream of the day I return to Gaza as a doctor and compensate it for everything it has endured.

Yes, the situation is difficult, and yes, the future is unclear, but I am Maram, a Tawjihi student from Gaza, and I still have hope.

Yes, life in Gaza is hard, full of challenges, but I believe that with willpower and determination, we can change. And we can achieve our dreams.

Date of Writing the Story: 2025/06/01

Safaa Qreqea

Age: 36 years

Original Place: Gaza

My name is Safaa Qreqea', and Allah forbid you see what we've seen. I'm a mother to children, and my only wish in life is their laughter. From the start of the war, displacement slaughtered us. Once here, once there, we searched for any place where we could find safety, but where is safety in Gaza?

Eventually, after months of wandering, we decided to return to northern Gaza. We thought, at least we'll die on our land. We found our house reduced to rubble, not a single stone left standing. What could we do? We pitched a tent in front of the destroyed house. We said, this is where we'll stay, among our stones, among our memories.

We lived in the tent for days, no water, no electricity, nothing. But we were happy, close to one another, feeling the scent of our homeland. But happiness didn't last long. They came to us and said we had to leave. Orders! Where should we go? It didn't matter where, just that we had to leave.

A person's heart dies a thousand deaths every day. Where should we go? Where should we find safety? We didn't know where to go, so we took our tent and a few belongings and went to a UNRWA school. The world was dark, cold, and fear gripped our hearts.

Here we are, sitting in the school, dozens of us crammed into a classroom. No privacy, no comfort. But thank Allah, there's a roof over our heads. My children are with me, and that's the most important thing. We pray to Allah to relieve us, to let us return to our home, even if it's rubble. The important thing is to return to our land, to our olive trees, to our shattered dreams. Allah is generous... Allah is generous.

Date of Writing the Story: 2025/06/01

173

Alaa Jundiya

Age: 28 years

Original Place: KhanYounis

I am Alaa, divorced with three children, Allah protect them. Allah forbid anyone from experiencing what we've seen in this war. From the first day of shelling, we left our homes and fled. If it weren't for my family, I would have been lost, Allah bless them. We set up a tent, just big enough to fit us.

My children were hungry; their stomachs growled from hunger. My heart broke for them. What could I do? The world stood still, no jobs, no opportunities. I told myself I had to figure something out to feed my children.

I started working in a clay oven, kneading and baking bread. The work was hard and backbreaking, but thank Allah, I was able to provide bread for my children to eat and fill their hunger. I was happy to see them eat with appetite, despite everything.

Happiness doesn't last long. A few days ago, we were ordered to evacuate. They said the area was dangerous, and we had to leave. Oh Allah, what kind of life is this? Running from death to death. We quickly packed our tent, grabbed our children and a few belongings, as much as we could carry.

Now we're displaced again, not knowing where to go or where to settle. But what I know for sure is that I'll remain strong for my children. I'll keep looking for any work to feed and protect them. Allah help each and every one of us, and may He relieve us and all of Gaza.

Date of Writing the Story: 2025/06/01

Inas Jundiya

Age: 36 years

Original Place: KhanYounis

I am Inas, a Gazan woman like all Gazan women. Allah help us through this life and its burdens. I have two daughters, Sama and Bara'a, beautiful as the moon, may Allah protect them. Life was going well by the grace of Allah until this war came and turned everything upside down.

We fled our home, like everyone else, leaving behind our world and memories. My family and siblings were all in the same situation, but my heart was broken, my other half wasn't there. My husband, the father of my daughters, stayed in the north. We begged him to come with us, but he refused. Allah be with him.

After a few weeks, we received news of his arrest. Oh Allah, what a disaster! The world turned black before my eyes, I didn't know what to do or where to go. For ten months, we were consumed with worry, not knowing if he was alive or dead. Every day, we prayed to Allah to give us news of him, and every night we slept with tears on our cheeks. Sama and Bara'a kept asking where their father had gone and why he hadn't returned. What could I tell them? My heart broke for them.

After all this suffering, thank Allah, the Red Cross informed us that he was detained. Oh, the joy that didn't last! Yes, he's detained, but at least he's alive and breathing. Thank Allah a thousand times.

Now we wait for the war to end, like everyone else. I want to see the father of my daughters safe, to return to the arms of his daughters and his home. I want to return to a normal life, even if simple, the important thing is that it's life. Oh Allah, Your relief is near. Oh Allah, return every missing person to their loved ones safely, and extinguish this war that has consumed our hearts.

We await the day we return to our homes, embrace our loved ones, and live in peace. Allah is generous.

Date of Writing the Story: 2025/06/01

Yasmeen Jundiya

Age: 36 years

Original Place: KhanYounis

I am Umm Ahmed, and this is my story in Gaza, Allah be with us. My husband, Abu Ahmed, Allah give him health, works odd jobs, sometimes he finds work, sometimes not. Life is hard, and prices are skyrocketing. So I told myself: "Woman, this can't continue. We need to support ourselves."

I thought and planned, what could I do? I'm a skilled homemaker, but I don't have a degree. After much thought, I remembered clay ovens. You know, those ovens where they bake traditional bread.

I told Abu Ahmed about my idea, but at first, he wasn't convinced. He said: "Woman, it's hard work, heat and fire, you won't handle it." But I insisted: "Try me, Abu Ahmed. You won't lose anything."

We found a small clay oven for rent in the Sha'af neighborhood after much difficulty. We agreed with the owner and paid monthly rent. We bought some flour, sesame seeds, and nigella seeds, and entrusted ourselves to Allah.

The first day was tough, the heat was intense, and the smoke suffocating, but I endured. I started kneading and baking, and the smell made mouths water. People began coming to buy, and thank Allah, they liked my bread.They started saying: "Umm Ahmed's bread is different, its taste reminds you of mothers' bread." That phrase meant the world to me.

The work isn't easy, it requires patience and perseverance. I wake up early before sunrise, prepare the dough, and light the oven. I bake all day, and when the last customer leaves, I clean the oven and prepare for the next day.

Sometimes Abu Ahmed helps me, he brings flour and collects wood, but his main job is to look for work. I don't get upset with him; I know he wants what's best for our children.

Thanks to the oven, we were able to pay off debts and buy some decent food for the kids. Sure, we don't spend much, but thank Allah, we're getting by. I'm Umm Ahmed, a simple Gazan woman, working in a clay oven, baking bread for people with love and honesty. Thank Allah for everything. Allah is generous, and tomorrow will be better.

Date of Writing the Story: 2025/06/01

Umm Ibrahim Jundiya

Age: 36 years

Original Place: KhanYounis

I am Umm Ahmed, and this is my story in Gaza, may Allah be with us. My husband, Abu Ahmed, may Allah give him health, works odd jobs, sometimes he finds work, sometimes not. Life is difficult, and prices are skyrocketing like fire. So I told myself, "Woman, this isn't right; we need to support ourselves."

I sat down to think and plan, what could I do? I'm a skilled homemaker, but I don't have a degree. After much thought, the idea of a clay oven came to mind. You know, those ovens where they bake traditional bread with that homey flavor.

I told Abu Ahmed about my idea, but at first, he wasn't convinced. He said, "Woman, this job is exhausting, with heat and fire, you won't handle it." But I insisted and told him, "Give me a try, Abu Ahmed. You won't lose anything."

We looked for a clay oven to rent, and with great difficulty, we found a small one in the Al-Shaaf neighborhood. We agreed with the owner and paid monthly rent. We bought some flour, sesame seeds, and nigella seeds, and entrusted ourselves to Allah.

The first day was tough, the heat was intense, and the smoke suffocating, but I endured. I started kneading and baking, and the smell made mouths water. People began coming to buy, and thank Allah, they liked my bread.

They started saying, "Umm Ahmed's bread is different, its taste reminds you of mothers' bread." That phrase meant the world to me.

The work isn't easy, it requires patience and perseverance. I wake up early before sunrise, prepare the dough, and light the oven. I bake all day, and when the last customer leaves, I clean the oven and get ready for the next day.

Sometimes Abu Ahmed helps me, he brings flour and collects wood, but his main job is to look for work. I don't get upset with him; I know he wants what's best for our children.

Thanks to the oven, we were able to pay off debts and buy some decent food for the kids. Sure, we don't spend much, but thank Allah, we're getting by.

I'm Umm Ahmed, a simple Gazan woman, working at a clay oven, baking bread for people with love and honesty. Thank Allah for everything. Allah is generous, and tomorrow will be better.

Date of Writing the Story: 2025/06/01

Story (124)

Suzan Obaid

Age: 36 years

Original Place: KhanYounis

Oh, the sorrow in my heart, no one knows what fate has in store. I'm Suzan, a daughter of this land. I married young and had Maged, the light of my eyes from my first husband. Things didn't work out between us, and we separated.

Later, Allah blessed me with another husband, I thought it was destiny, and I wanted to move on with my life. But then, this war came, leaving no one untouched. We fled our home, like everyone else, and oh, how hard displacement is, and how terrifying it is to fear for your children. We stayed in a tent, day after day, waiting for relief. The sun burns, and the cold stings, but the hope in our hearts never faded.

When they said we could return to the north, we rejoiced with a happiness unmatched. We thought, "Finally, the nightmare is over." But oh, how I wish we hadn't returned. Oh, how I wish we hadn't seen what became of our home. Everything was gone, everything destroyed. Our land was scorched, and our house wasn't there anymore, it was in an area we weren't allowed to return to.

What could we do? Where could we go? We said, "We have no one but Allah." We brought a tent and pitched it next to our land, which was once our home. We stayed there, me, my husband, and my children. The tent became our whole world. We wait, and we pray to Allah to relieve us and all these people who are helpless. We wait for safety, and we wait for a better future for Maged. We wait... but we don't know for what.

Date of Writing the Story: 2025/06/01

Umm Salem

Age: 56 years

Original Place: Gaza

From the first day the war began, I felt like the world was going to turn upside down on us. It wasn't my first time experiencing war, but this time was different, terrifying in a way I can't describe. I was sitting with my husband and five children, the youngest just two years old, when the first sound of shelling rang out. My heart sank with fear, but I hid my trembling and said, "I have to stay strong, for them."

As soon as we heard our neighborhood was no longer safe, we grabbed a few belongings and sought refuge at my sister's house. We didn't stay there long, just a week, because the shelling grew closer and closer, so we decided to flee to a government school. The first night, we slept on the floor, no mattress, no blanket, and the cold bit us from above and below. I hugged my children, buried my face in their chests, and said, "We're okay here, we're together."

Every day, I tried to create a sense of normalcy for them, I'd tell them stories, cook for them, even if it was just plain rice without oil, just so we'd feel like we weren't alone. After a week, they told us we had to leave the school. I gathered our things, carried my youngest on my shoulder, and walked with the crowd, thousands of us, all faces filled with fear. After much hardship, we reached the south and set up a small tent. It was the fourth tent we'd started from scratch.

I'd cook lentils for my children, boil water, sprinkle salt, and stir with a wooden spoon. It felt like I was preparing a grand feast, but in reality, I just wanted to feed them something to make them forget hunger and humiliation.

We lived in four tents, and each time, we tried to settle in, cleaning, hanging pictures, putting up fresh sheets. But everything was temporary. One day we'd be forced to move, another day bombs would fall nearby, and another day we'd lose someone we knew.

One time, while brushing my youngest daughter's hair, I heard a loud, nearby explosion. The girls screamed, and my little boy wet himself from fear. I hugged them close, hiding them in my chest, and said in a broken voice, "I'm with you… no one will come near you as long as I'm alive."

A few days later, I received news of my cousin's son being martyred. The news hit me like a stone on my chest. I wiped my tears quickly, calmed my children, and said, "May Allah have mercy on him... he's a martyr, and he's gone to paradise."

Every day, I'd wake up before dawn, clean around the tent, pray, and make supplications: "Oh Allah, bring us back to our home. Let us drink coffee again on the tiles of our house, open our windows, and breathe the scent of the sea, not the scent of fear."

One day, my daughter drew our house on an old cardboard box and wrote above it, "Return is near." I hung it on the tent wall and said, "This isn't a dream... it's a promise."

Date of Writing the Story: 2025/06/01

Elham Al-Othmani

Age: 30 years

I am Elham, from northern Gaza, I wish I had never left. I'm displaced with my four children in the south, oh, the sorrow of the south. We live in a tent, like thousands of others. I'm married, and I have four children, Allah protect them. A week ago, I gave birth to a baby girl, as beautiful as the moon, but I haven't named her yet. My soul feels heavy.

During childbirth, I had a hemorrhage. The world spun around me, I didn't know where I was going. They took me to the hospital, gave me blood and plasma transfusions. My health was at its lowest point. The reason? Poor nutrition, oh, the sorrow. Lack of food. In Gaza, people, you can't find a bite to fill your stomach.

Our situation is very difficult, extremely so. We don't have food or even the medications we needed. Prices are skyrocketing, burning us alive. Even for the newborn, I adore her, I couldn't afford clothes, milk, or even diapers.

You feel paralyzed, unable to do anything. All I want is to see my daughter wearing clean clothes, fed and satisfied. All I want is for my children to sleep with full bellies. All I want... oh, all I want is to return to our homes and live with dignity.

I just wish... I wish someone would hear our voices, understand our pain. I wish someone would help us, not to live in luxury, but to live with dignity, to eat, drink, and keep our children warm. I wish... I wish, oh world, that someone is listening.

Date of Writing the Story: 2025/06/01

Iman Salouha

Age: 29 years

Original Place: Al-Zaytoun

I am a mother, a widow, and my name is Iman Salouha. The war on Gaza changed every detail of my life and broke things that will never return to how they were. My husband was martyred during the aggression, he was my pillar, my rock, the father of my children, and the protector of my daughters, whom I now care for in every detail.

We lived a simple life, but it was full of warmth and love, even though life around us was hard. He always told me, "Life doesn't stop, we keep trying." And he truly did try, he worked, cared for the house, and reassured us even when he was tired.

But the war took him… we couldn't say goodbye, and I couldn't tell him my final words. His soul departed, and I was left behind. From that day on, the responsibility on my shoulders became greater than I could bear, but I refused to give up.

I became both mother and father, friend, and storyteller before bedtime. My youngest daughter used to ask me, "Mommy, where is Daddy?" And I'd answer, "Daddy is in paradise… he's praying for us from there." She may not fully understand, but my embrace became her safe haven.

Today, I care for my daughters, teaching them, raising them, protecting them, and planting strength within them, even though inside, I'm broken. I do the impossible to ensure they don't feel orphaned, to make them know they're not alone, and that their mother stands firm for them.

Life is hard, but we are tougher. Those who've lived in Gaza and experienced war know what it means to be strong against all odds. But I, Iman, will not weaken. I will continue this path, for them, and for his pure soul watching over us from above.

Date of Writing the Story: 2025/06/01

Umm Abdullah

Age: 36 years

Original Place: KhanYounis

I am Umm Abdullah... and this is my story, the one I never dreamed of living.

The world was night, not just by the hour... but night in my life. The sound of shelling never stopped, and every minute felt like a year.

We fled to my in-laws' house, but my heart wasn't at peace. Hussein, my husband, refused to leave with us. He held my hand and said with unwavering confidence:

"I won't leave my home... no matter what happens."

I begged him, saying, "Hussein, think of Abdullah... think of me"!

He shook his head and replied:

"If we all leave, who will guard these walls? Who will protect the memories"?

And so we left... and I left him behind, though my heart stayed with him.

A week passed. Every day, I woke up to news and went to sleep haunted by fear. My heart was restless every moment. Until that day came, the day that broke me forever.

I learned that Hussein had decided to go see our house in the Al-Montar neighborhood. Al-Montar was the most dangerous area at the time, a battlefield of death. I thought to myself, "It's impossible... Hussein is there"?

Before I could process it, the news arrived like a knife cutting through me:

A reconnaissance drone struck him and his cousin... and they were martyred.

Six others were injured, and their blood soaked the ground.

I imagined him standing in front of our house, looking at the rubble, maybe smiling and saying, "There's still hope we can rebuild."

But the drone didn't give him a chance, not even to say goodbye.

I cried, screamed, prayed, but the pain remained silent... settled deep within me.

Since then, I became both mother and father to Abdullah. I hold him as if I'm holding Hussein. Every night, I pray to Allah to comfort me, even if only in my dreams.

Hussein didn't die... Hussein lives on inside me, in his son, in every memory, in every laugh we shared amidst the terror.

Date of Writing the Story: 2025/06/01

Marwa Omar Mohammad Al-Ghaseen

Age: 36 years

Original Place: KhanYounis

I am Marwa Al-Ghaseen, from Gaza... from the heart of the rubble that has become a home.

Our house, which once held laughter and warmth, turned into rubble. When it was hit, nothing remained but dust, smoke, and shock. We had nowhere to go but the streets, so we pitched a small tent among the ruins, thinking we might continue life somehow. That tent became our home, our kitchen, our bedroom, and even our hospital.

My husband is sick, sitting all day, exhausted and silent, not because he chose silence, but because when pain grows too heavy, it consumes everything, even vitality. There's no work, no source of income, and I've become the one who must move for everyone.

My children... when I look into their eyes, I see something greater than childhood. I see hunger, exhaustion, and waiting. Many times, we sit in front of a plate of rice, and each pretends to be full so the others can have more.

Once, my daughter asked for a bag of chips... She looked at me with brokenness deeper than her small hands, and my heart was too weak to respond.

At night, the cold comes like a monster... the tent shakes with every gust of wind, and the whistling sound of plastic has become part of our stories. We wrap the kids in an old sheet, and I tell them from memory: "There was a house... and a door... and warmth."

The water? It tastes salty, murky, but we drink it. We have no choice. Our stomachs have grown accustomed to bitterness, and my children's bodies have grown thin from malnutrition, yet their spirits still try to laugh.

My youngest son doesn't walk... as if the war took his legs and left him behind. I carry him in my arms and take steps for him, telling him: "One day you'll fly, not just walk."

I am not a story. I am not a number.

I am a mother, a wife, a tent, and a loaf of bread divided among four.

I am Gaza... and today, I still stand on my feet, even if the whole world has fallen around me.

Date of Writing the Story: 2025/06/01

Nermeen Farahat

Age: 32 years

Original Place: Al-Zaytoun

I am Nermeen, from Gaza... I became a widow five years ago when my husband passed away, may Allah have mercy on him. He entrusted me with our daughters, and since then, I've been both mother and father to them.

Life isn't easy, but when the war came, it became harder than imagination. We fled our home, carrying only a few belongings, hearts full of fear. And I carried the burden of worry for my daughters, one small, the other a bit older. From the first day of displacement, I held myself together, trying to stay strong for them. Inside the tent, there's no privacy: no food, no safety, no peace... but I smiled in front of them and hid my tears under the blanket. I told them: "Everything will pass, Mommy. We're strong, aren't we? Isn't that what Grandma always said"?

I cooked lentils or a little rice over a small fire, simple meals, but we ate them together as if they were banquets. Whenever one of them got sick, I ran to find medicine, but often found none.

The burden is heavy, people... being alone with my daughters in such conditions, war, shelling, displacement, and scarcity of everything. But I say: "Oh Allah, keep me standing for them. I don't want anything except to see them safe."

I am Nermeen, the mother of my daughters... Maybe I'm alone, but Allah is with me, and my daughters are my strength. The war stole much from us, but their embrace gives me back everything.

Date of Writing the Story: 2025/06/01

Mushira Al-Harazeen

Age: 30 years

Original Place: Gaza

I am Umm Ahmed, and this is my story in Gaza, Allah be with us. My husband, Abu Ahmed, may Allah grant him health, works odd jobs, sometimes he finds work, sometimes not. Life is difficult, and prices are skyrocketing like fire. So I told myself, "Woman, this isn't right; we need to support ourselves."

I sat down to think and plan, what could I do? I'm a skilled homemaker, but I don't have a degree. After much thought, the idea of a clay oven came to mind. You know, those ovens where they bake traditional bread with that homey flavor.

I told Abu Ahmed about my idea, but at first, he wasn't convinced. He said, "Woman, this job is exhausting, with heat and fire, you won't handle it." But I insisted and told him, "Give me a try, Abu Ahmed. You won't lose anything."

We looked for a clay oven to rent, and with great difficulty, we found a small one in the Al-Shaaf neighborhood. We agreed with the owner and paid monthly rent. We bought some flour, sesame seeds, and nigella seeds, and entrusted ourselves to Allah.

The first day was tough, the heat was intense, and the smoke suffocating, but I endured. I started kneading and baking, and the smell made mouths water. People began coming to buy, and thank Allah, they liked my bread.

They started saying, "Umm Ahmed's bread is different, its taste reminds you of mothers' bread." That phrase meant the world to me.

The work isn't easy, it requires patience and perseverance. I wake up early before sunrise, prepare the dough, and light the oven. I bake all day, and when the last customer leaves, I clean the oven and get ready for the next day.

Sometimes Abu Ahmed helps me, he brings flour and collects wood, but his main job is to look for work. I don't get upset with him; I know he wants what's best for our children.

Thanks to the oven, we were able to pay off debts and buy some decent food for the kids. Sure, we don't spend much, but thank Allah, we're getting by.

I'm Umm Ahmed, a simple Gazan woman, working at a clay oven, baking bread for people with love and honesty. Thank Allah for everything. Allah is generous, and tomorrow will be better.

Date of Writing the Story: 2025/06/01

Waad Al-Harazeen

Age: 20 years

Original Place: Al-Zaytoun

I am Umm Ahmed, and this is my story in Gaza, Allah be with us. My husband, Abu Ahmed, may Allah grant him health, works odd jobs, sometimes he finds work, sometimes not. Life is difficult, and prices are skyrocketing like fire. So I told myself, "Woman, this isn't right; we need to support ourselves."

I sat down to think and plan, what could I do? I'm a skilled homemaker, but I don't have a degree. After much thought, the idea of a clay oven came to mind. You know, those ovens where they bake traditional bread with that homey flavor.

I told Abu Ahmed about my idea, but at first, he wasn't convinced. He said, "Woman, this job is exhausting, with heat and fire, you won't handle it." But I insisted and told him, "Give me a try, Abu Ahmed. You won't lose anything."

We looked for a clay oven to rent, and with great difficulty, we found a small one in the Al-Shaaf neighborhood. We agreed with the owner and paid monthly rent. We bought some flour, sesame seeds, and nigella seeds, and entrusted ourselves to Allah.

The first day was tough, the heat was intense, and the smoke suffocating, but I endured. I started kneading and baking, and the smell made mouths water. People began coming to buy, and thank Allah, they liked my bread.

They started saying, "Umm Ahmed's bread is different, its taste reminds you of mothers' bread." That phrase meant the world to me.

The work isn't easy, it requires patience and perseverance. I wake up early before sunrise, prepare the dough, and light the oven. I bake all day, and when the last customer leaves, I clean the oven and get ready for the next day.

Sometimes Abu Ahmed helps me, he brings flour and collects wood, but his main job is to look for work. I don't get upset with him; I know he wants what's best for our children.

Thanks to the oven, we were able to pay off debts and buy some decent food for the kids. Sure, we don't spend much, but thank Allah, we're getting by.

I'm Umm Ahmed, a simple Gazan woman, working at a clay oven, baking bread for people with love and honesty. Thank Allah for everything. Allah is generous, and tomorrow will be better.

Date of Writing the Story: 2025/06/01

Umm Qusay

Age: 59 years

I am Umm Qusay, and I raised five sons and three married daughters. My entire life revolved around them, they are the source of my pride and strength. But fate was not kind; it took so much from me. My eldest son became a martyr, and his brother also fell in Gaza's revolution, in the battle of truth and resilience.

Hunger and patience became our daily weapons, not just fighting on the battlefield but resisting through survival, enduring despite all harsh conditions. When I say "resistance," I don't mean weapons, I mean the human will to endure the cruelty of life, to hold your heart and resist hunger, cold, and endless pain.

I remember the cold winter nights when the electricity would cut off for days, and the cold would bite my children's bones. I tried to warm them with old blankets, but their hearts were more tired than their bodies. They would ask me, "Mom, why is there no food? Why aren't we warm?" And my heart would break as I answered in a broken voice, "Patience, my children, patience."

Once, a neighbor brought us some bread and a little lentil stew. He said, "Oh, Umm Qusay, we fight hunger together; we must stick together." I felt I wasn't alone, that many others were enduring with me. Even my young sons, despite their pain and loss, never left the front lines. Once, my son returned from battle, his body exhausted, but his eyes burned with hope and determination. He said, "Mom, we protect the land, even if hunger kills us, we won't surrender." I was proud yet tearful, knowing they bore more than I ever could.

One time, life closed in on me. I didn't even have money to buy medicine for my youngest daughter, whose health was deteriorating day by day. I cried silently and told myself, "You must be strong, you must endure." From then on, every time life reminded me of its wounds, I remembered that this hunger we fight isn't just about lack of food, it's a battle for survival and patience.

Even when we waited in long lines for aid distribution, I saw the faces of weary people, all resisting their hunger and pain. Sometimes my children would see others waiting hours for a piece of bread and learn patience from those around them.

I am Umm Qusay, resisting every pain and hunger pang, every tear of patience, and every hardship I endure, it's all a testament to my resilience. This hunger we suffer isn't just about losing a meal; it's a cry of patience against the occupation trying to kill us. But we are stronger than all circumstances, and we endure.

And I truly believe that this patience, this resistance through hunger and endurance, is what keeps our spirits alive. Our tears, pain, and martyrs will remain a light in Gaza's darkness, and our patience is the strongest weapon against injustice.

Date of Writing the Story: 2025/06/01

Randa Fathi Ahmad Zemmo

Age: 36 years

Original Place: Rimal

Place of Displacement: Thalatheeni Street

Our old house near Canal Street, close to Dawoud building, was bombed during the war, and we had to leave quickly, moving to live near the old power plant on Thalatheeni Street.

My husband has been suffering from general weakness due to malnutrition and can no longer move easily. I remember the day he tried to bring us water from afar but collapsed from exhaustion. I sat beside him crying, unsure how to help him.

In the small tent we now live in, there's no electricity or heating, and the cold and heat worsen our suffering. My young children have begun to understand our struggles. Once, my youngest daughter brought stale bread, divided it among us, and said, "Dad needs to eat with me."

The day the shelling got too close to our old house, we ran to save ourselves. I carried my sick husband while fleeing with the family, not knowing if we'd make it safely.

The circumstances are tough, but we keep moving forward, one step at a time, enduring whatever fate throws at us.

Date of Writing the Story: 2025/06/01

Fidaa

Age: 38 years

I am Fidaa, the mother of Mohammad, a boy with autism. Since his birth, my entire life has revolved around him. I love him and try to understand and support him as much as I can. Life hasn't been easy, but raising a child with special needs has made it infinitely harder, especially here in the tents.

When we fled our home, everything felt like fog and darkness. The heat, sun, and humidity only added to the misery, and Mohammad struggled to adapt. The tent is cramped, offering no space for calm or comfort. Mohammad can't cope with noise or crowds, and any loud sound makes him anxious and causes him to scream.

Every morning, I wake up before everyone else to prepare a quiet, organized space for him. I bring simple toys to help him focus because when he gets overwhelmed, he screams and cries, and it's hard to calm him. Sometimes I sleep next to him on the ground in the tent because he seems to need my constant presence.

Life in the tent is hard. At night, it's freezing, and Mohammad feels the cold quickly, disrupting his sleep. Even on hot days, the heat tires and agitates him. I try to cool him with cold water or use a small fan, but these solutions barely meet his real needs.

People around us try to help, but everyone has their own struggles. Often, I feel alone under the immense responsibility. My other children also try to assist, but Mohammad consumes all my time and energy, especially during his sudden meltdowns.

Mohammad's medical challenges are numerous, and sometimes I need to take him to clinics or doctors. But traveling is difficult and dangerous due to the war and siege. Sometimes I can't reach my destination because of fuel shortages or blocked roads. My heart breaks watching him suffer without being able to ease his pain.

Still, I refuse to give up. I strive to learn more about his condition, reading books and watching videos to better understand how to care for him. I create a consistent routine to help him find calm, even amidst chaos.

Life in the tents is tough, but Mohammad is my source of strength. For him, I rise each day, trying to create moments of peace and joy amid the destruction. Though we don't live in a beautiful house or lead normal lives, my presence and care for him are our only hope.

Date of Writing the Story: 2025/06/01

Majida Al-Turk

Original Place: Al-Shati Camp

Place of Displacement: Nasser Street

I am Majida Omar Mohammad Turk, from Gaza, and our family consists of seven members. My husband, Bahaa, suffers from three herniated discs in his back and cannot work due to severe pain. I have three daughters, all diagnosed with thalassemia, requiring lifelong treatment.

The war has deeply affected us, not just through destruction and fear but also in securing medication and treatment. Many times, we've searched pharmacies and clinics, only to hear there's none available or that it's prohibitively expensive.

I remember the day shells approached our home. I clutched my daughters' medications tightly as they cried in fear, and Bahaa, despite his pain, tried to comfort them.

Once, we had to travel to a distant hospital because the nearby clinic had been bombed. Bahaa, already weak, struggled to walk. I accompanied him and our children through slow, painful steps, navigating streets filled with rubble and panicked people.

We slept on the floor in a small shelter, waking repeatedly to the sounds of shelling. Our youngest daughter suffered from severe anemia and urgently needed a blood transfusion. I visited dozens of hospitals, but all were either full or out of supplies. My heart shattered as I listened to her cries.

Despite all the suffering and difficulties, we endure, clinging to each other. Every day, I pray for relief and healing for my children.

Date of Writing the Story: 2025/06/01

Rawda Mahmoud Abu Harbeed

Age: 36 years

Original Place: Beit Hanoun

Place of Displacement: Islamic University, Gaza

I am Rawda Mahmoud Abu Harbeed, a widow from Gaza, and my family includes four members. Before the war, we lived in Beit Hanoun among relatives and neighbors. Despite life's hardships, we tried to live peacefully. But as the shelling intensified, our home became a target. Explosions grew closer daily, forcing us to leave before it was too late.

We moved to a small, cramped house near the Islamic University, far from our loved ones. The new place was cold, and conditions worsened, especially for my three daughters, who suffer from thalassemia. Watching them undergo regular blood transfusions breaks my heart, but I can only do so much to secure their medications. Amidst the blockade and crisis, things aren't easy.

I recall the nights of heavy shelling when the earth shook, and my heart raced. My frightened children cried, and though I tried to console them, I was terrified too, scared for their future and safety. We huddled together on the cold floor, covered by a thin blanket that barely shielded us from the biting cold.

One day, my youngest complained of stomach pain and needed immediate medical attention. But the road was blocked due to shelling. The journey was perilous, and my fear knew no bounds. I walked with him through ruined streets, each blast piercing my ears, praying for his safety.

My late husband, Bahaa, suffered from chronic back pain and couldn't work. Now, I bear the responsibility of caring for my daughters and ensuring their survival in unimaginable circumstances. There are moments when I feel overwhelmed, but seeing my daughters' pain gives me the strength to persevere.

One particularly intense night, shelling damaged our new home. Part of the roof collapsed, filling the air with screams and panic. I gathered my children quickly, feeling my heart shatter but knowing I had to stay strong for them. I hide my fears for their sake, but when alone, the tears flow uncontrollably.

Even running errands feels like an adventure, every step fraught with danger. Yet, for my children, I'm willing to endure anything.

Despite all the pain and hardship, I strive to remain patient and resilient. I remind myself: These moments are difficult, but they won't last forever. I want to provide my children with a better life, a life of peace and security, even if the road ahead is long.

Date of Writing the Story: 2025/06/01

Amal Asaad Abdul Aziz

Original Place: Jabalia

Place of Displacement: Sweidi Al-Nasr

I am Amal Asaad Hassan Abdul Aziz, my husband is Ibrahim Omar Hussein Al-Far, and I live with our three children near Sweidi Al-Nasr after leaving our old home in Jabalia, in the Al-Almi Project. Life has changed significantly due to the war, and every day we face new challenges.

At the beginning of our displacement, the situation was extremely difficult. We were sleeping while terrified by the continuous sounds of shelling, and the children didn't understand why we had to leave our home and daily lives. Once, as we were trying to organize our belongings, we heard a loud explosion nearby, and everyone started running frantically. I carried my youngest child to calm him down while his older siblings tried to help and keep things organized.

Our old house in Jabalia was full of memories. But when the shelling became intense, we decided to leave it and head to Sweidi Al-Nasr, which we thought would be relatively safe. Despite the hardships here, Ibrahim and I try to provide our children with as normal a life as possible and hold onto hope despite the exhaustion and fear.

Every day, I hear the sounds of shelling and worry about my family's safety. But I tell myself that I must be patient and strong for my children. Ibrahim is a patient man who strengthens me, and together, we support each other to face everything.

The days of displacement, when we left our home in Beit Hanoun, were incredibly hard. The house where I raised my children became rubble. What was once a refuge and comfort turned into a painful memory. We were forced to live in a cramped space, far from everything familiar. Despite all this, we remain resilient, living with hope for tomorrow.

These days are tough on all of us, but hope for life and peace remains in our hearts.

Date of Writing the Story: 2025/06/01

Wessal Zuhair Sahweel

Original Place: Beit Hanoun

Place of Displacement: Gaza

I am Wessal, a wife and mother of six children. Before the war, life was difficult, but we endured everything together. My husband, Ahmed, suffers from a herniated disc in his back; the pain is constant, making it hard for him to move or work. I have issues with my electrical system, meaning we often need medication and treatment, but we don't always find or afford them.

Before the war, we lived in Beit Hanoun among our relatives and neighbors, who became like an extended family. Our house was simple but a shelter and a haven for my children. However, when the shelling intensified, our home became unsafe. Every day, we heard explosions, and every night, we feared closing our eyes, worried about our children. We were forced to leave our home and come to Gaza, even though the situation wasn't better. We were searching for temporary safety.

The room we live in now is small, and its tightness pains my heart. With six children and our illnesses, life has become much harder. The children are young and need a lot, and I'm scared for them, especially with my illness and my husband's condition, which increases our worries. Sometimes, I wait hours to get medicine, and sometimes we can't find it. My heart breaks when I see my children suffering due to a lack of healthcare.

I remember one time when the electricity was cut off for more than three days, and the cold was biting. The house felt like a freezer. The children were shivering, and our conditions worsened with every moment spent without warmth. I tried to cover them with blankets, but there was a persistent fear and anxiety in my heart. My husband, despite his pain, tried to comfort me, encouraging me with kind words or a simple laugh. He worked as much as he could, but the pain made it hard for him to move easily.

Once, our neighbor brought us a piece of bread and gave it to me for my children. It felt like a priceless treasure at the time. When I saw my children eating that bread, tears rolled down my cheeks, tears of weakness, mixed with bitter joy. It was a brief moment, but it meant so much to us amid this hell.

The war doesn't stop, and the pain, hunger, and illness only increase. My responsibilities as a mother, a friend to my husband, and a caregiver to my children have multiplied. But no matter how hard things get, I remind myself: "We must be patient, we must endure, for our children, for our lives, for our hope."

I am a mother. The tear I wipe from my son's eye, the words I say to my little daughter, I tell them: "No matter what happens, we are a family. We are resilient. We resist, and this is our path." I pray to Allah every day to protect my children, ease my burdens and my husband's, and give us the patience and strength to continue.

Date of Writing the Story: 2025/06/01

Story (140)

Salwa Zaki Abu Haloub

Original Place: Beit Lahiya

I am Salwa Zaki Mahmoud Abu Haloub, a mother of nine children, four of whom require special care due to their illnesses. We lived in Beit Lahiya, but after the war, our house was destroyed and became uninhabitable. We were forced to flee to the Al-Nasr neighborhood, near the Sharia court, where we began a new life amidst difficult circumstances.

My eldest son is quadriplegic and requires round-the-clock care. I change his diapers, help him eat, and take care of every detail of his life, even when I'm exhausted. Sometimes, I hear his cries of pain, and my heart breaks because I can't do anything but pray and endure. My second son is deaf and mute but incredibly intelligent, bringing me joy despite his struggles. My daughter battles cancer, and every day is a new fight, between treatments, fatigue, and pain. My father lost his sight after an injury and can no longer work, leaving the entire family's responsibility on my shoulders.

During winter, despite the freezing cold and few blankets, we struggle to keep warm in our small house. Sometimes, we place covers over broken windows to shield ourselves from the icy wind. My heart aches every time I see my children's faces frozen from the cold.

One day, a neighbor brought us a bag of firewood. He stood at our door and said, "This is the least we can offer you." Tears filled my eyes, and I felt a glimmer of hope amid the darkness. That's how people here are, even after all they've been through, they still give and support one another.

Sometimes, I let my children play outside in the nearby street despite the surrounding danger, just so they can feel normal for a moment and experience their childhood despite everything. I watch them from afar as they laugh and play, praying that Allah protects them from the horrors of war and harsh circumstances.

Many nights, I stay awake, watching over my sick children, fearing any deterioration in their condition. Sometimes, I hear the sound of nearby explosions and gather them in a corner of the house to reassure them. But my heart fills with indescribable fear and worry.

My life is full of pain and suffering, but I refuse to give up. I am a mother, responsible for my family and my children, who are my entire life. Despite everything we go through, I believe that patience and faith are the way to rise again.

The war didn't just take my home, it took part of my life and childhood. But it didn't take my strength or determination to keep going. My hope is that one day we will return to our home and build a new life, one filled with safety and happiness for my children.

Date of Writing the Story: 2025/06/01

Story (141)

Umm Shadi

I am Umm Shadi, an elderly mother with a large family. I have five sons and three married daughters. My eldest son and his cousin were martyred in the war, but I remain patient and accept Allah's will. The pain in my heart is immense, but faith and patience are what keep me going.

The war has destroyed everything around us, and every day brings news of the loss of loved ones and dear friends. My young sons never surrendered; instead, many joined the resistance to defend their homeland and protect our people. My sons always told me: "Mother, there's no choice but to persevere. Resistance is our duty, and defending our land is our honor."

I'm proud of them, despite the fear that fills my heart whenever they go out to fight. Each time they return, I hear stories of their bravery and sacrifices. But I also fear for them every time, praying to Allah to protect them and give them strength.

One day, my eldest son went on a mission with his comrades. The conditions were dire, the shelling didn't stop, and the night was pitch black. But they were determined to defend, even if it cost them their lives. When I heard the news of his martyrdom, my heart shattered, but I told myself I had to be strong for my children and daughters.

As a mother, I live with pain every day, but patience and faith in Allah are my weapons to protect myself. Hunger, poverty, and the difficulties of life in Gaza have become part of my daily resistance. Every small meal and every moment of patience is a form of struggle.

Even my married daughters, despite their responsibilities and hardships, supported their families and stood by us. In our family, we remain united despite the pain, and each of us does what we can to preserve dignity and pride.

I am Umm Shadi, and I say to every mother in Gaza: We don't just endure, we resist through our hunger, sorrow, and strength. Every moment of patience is a victory, and every tear is a testimony.

Date of Writing the Story: 2025/06/01

Raeda Ziad Kaskin

Age: 35 years

Place of Displacement: Barcelona Park

Profession: Teacher

A Story of Displacement and Unforgettable Pain

On October 7, 2023, a Saturday, my weekly day off from school, I woke up startled by deafening sounds shaking the area. At first, I thought it was thunder, never imagining it could be missiles, so I went back to sleep until 8 a.m. When I woke up again, I realized something wasn't right. The noise outside, the strange commotion, the unbearable atmosphere, I asked my mother and siblings in fear: "Is this a dream? Thunder? Or what's happening?"

I rushed to the TV to understand what was going on, and there it was... a shock beyond belief. The war had begun, and the pain came early, we received news that two of our cousins had been martyred. My heart shattered, and with every new report, fear grew stronger and terror intensified. Our house is close to the sea, and Israeli naval forces were continuously firing into the waters.

We fled to my grandfather's house seeking safety, then returned home, but we didn't stay long. We received calls from the occupation ordering us to move 500 meters away from the sea, so we moved to my sister's house on the next street. From there, the shelling intensified over the Al-Karama area, and red flares lit up the sky above us. I trembled with fear, crying nonstop, unsure of what awaited us.

On October 13, 2023, we decided to flee to the Al-Shifa neighborhood. We ran, carrying whatever belongings we could, in an unforgettable scene. Afterward, we headed to my sister's house in Nuseirat. We stayed there for five months, enduring hunger, displacement, and daily hardships. There wasn't enough water, so we carried it ourselves, cooked over open fires, and got food from distribution centers. Amidst all this, another devastating blow struck, news of my eldest brother's martyrdom. We couldn't imagine losing him, and the wound deepened when his eldest son was also injured.

After my brother's martyrdom, his family came to live with us in my sister's house. We became 45 people living in one home! An unbearable scene. No water, no electricity, no food, yet we tried to endure.

The shelling didn't stop, and destruction followed us everywhere. We had to flee again, heading to Rafah, where we lived in tents for five more months, suffering through the freezing winter cold and the suffocating summer heat. Flies and insects were everywhere, sand crept into everything. We carried water, waited in long lines at distribution centers, and faced daily struggles just to survive.

After those five months, we returned to Nuseirat. The same fear, poverty, and hunger remained. Not enough food, no money to buy anything. Water was purchased, bread came from long queues, and life became a constant struggle for survival.

After four more months, we finally returned to our home in Al-Shati. But what we found wasn't a house in the true sense, no windows, no doors, no furniture, nothing to protect us. The house was completely destroyed, yet we decided to repair it as best we could and settled there. The same suffering persisted: lack of food, difficulty obtaining clothing and drinkable water, and relentless fear.

We've been displaced multiple times and hosted displaced families many times, trying to live and keep going despite the pain inside us. Praise be to Allah in every situation; we thank Him always and pray He changes our condition for the better. Today, I live with new hope, I wait for the border to open, hoping I can travel to find some rest and safety, perhaps finding there what I haven't found here, hoping life will open another door to lighten this burden that has never left me.

Date of Writing the Story: 2025/06/01

Israa

Age: 25 years

Original Place: Gaza

A Nurse Between Death and Survival

I am Israa, a nurse from Gaza. In my work, I'm used to being strong, holding patients' hands, comforting them, and standing by them during their pain. But what we experienced starting October 7, 2023, was unlike any pain we'd ever known, neither in the hospital nor in our lives.

That day, I was returning from my night shift at Al-Shifa Hospital, exhausted and planning to get a few hours of sleep. Suddenly, I heard a massive explosion shake the house to its foundation. At first, I thought it was a regular explosion like the ones we hear often, but when I saw terrified faces and phones ringing incessantly, I knew it was something bigger.

We turned on the TV, and the disaster unfolded... the war had begun. All of Gaza became a target; every street and every home was threatened. The hospital called: "Israa, we need you. The emergency room is full of casualties." I dressed quickly and ran without thinking. The road to the hospital was filled with smoke, people running, crying children, and bodies lying on the ground. I couldn't believe this was my workplace and reality.

In the first days of the war, I worked 18-hour shifts, sometimes more. Deep wounds, amputated limbs, people dying while we tried desperately to save them. Between cases, I would go to the bathroom, cry, wipe my tears, and return to work as if nothing happened.

But after a few days, things worsened further, and threats reached our home in Tel Al-Hawa. On October 13, we received an evacuation order telling us to leave immediately. I gathered my mother, younger sister, and nephews, leaving everything behind. We fled to my uncle's place in Nuseirat. About two weeks later, the house we had fled was bombed... had we delayed by even one day, we would have been under the rubble.

In Nuseirat, conditions were tough. I volunteered at the nearest medical center during the day and returned late at night to find my mother cooking over a stone fire and my sister washing clothes by hand. There was no water, gas, or electricity. When the shelling intensified, we fled again to Rafah.

We lived in a tent among hundreds of others, no proper toilets, no privacy, no sleep. In the cold, we huddled together to stay warm, and in the heat, we placed wet cloths on our heads. Flies were relentless, and people collapsed from exhaustion. Amidst all this suffering, the field hospital in Rafah called, asking me to return to work with them.

I put on my white coat again, but my heart wasn't light, it was heavy with grief and despair. Once, a young man arrived injured, screaming: "Where's my mom? Where's my sister?" He didn't know they had been martyred in the same attack. I tried to hold his hand and comfort him, but I couldn't, my tears fell before his did.

Every day, I returned to the tent exhausted, carrying bread, some food, and trying to smile for my family, saying: "Tomorrow will be better," but inside, my heart was breaking.

After five months in Rafah, we returned to Nuseirat, but the situation hadn't improved. The market was empty, people were weary, and I felt I had lost myself after witnessing so much pain. Four months later, we decided to return to our home in Tel Al-Hawa. The house was destroyed, no windows, no doors, no bed, no pots. But we said: "Thank Allah for the little we have; we're back on our land." Slowly, we began rebuilding life: cleaning, hanging sheets over broken windows, cooking outside, and waiting for any aid to arrive.

Today, sitting amidst this destruction, my heart is full of prayers, for my family, for the patients, for the martyrs, and for every mother who lost her child. And still, I have hope, despite the exhaustion, the nightmares, and the oppression.

I now wait for the border to open, hoping I can travel to Libya to continue my work there, to feel like a nurse not just for the wounds of war but for life itself, a life filled with hope and peace. I dream of a room with a clean bed, a patient smiling at me, and simply... safety.

No matter what happens, I'll remain proud to be a nurse from Gaza, holding onto life, even if it feels broken.

Date of Writing the Story: 2025/06/01

Aya Yasser Al-Muqaied

Age: 24 yearsOriginal Place: Jabalia

Place of Displacement: Nuseirat

Aya Who Vanished, Yet Her Presence Remains

Aya wasn't an ordinary girl; she was extraordinary. She radiated hope and intelligence, and everyone who knew her said: "She's going to make us proud." Aya was a software engineer, brilliant in an extraordinary way. I don't just mean brilliant because she got good grades, but because she loved what she did with all her heart. Just a week before the war, she entered her fifth year, the graduation year, and ranked second in her class. We dreamed together of pursuing further studies and founding a software company. She used to say: "Dana, I want to create an app to help people who lost limbs in the war." She saw beyond a mere degree; she envisioned making an impact on people's lives.

Two months before the war, Aya got engaged to a respectable, cultured dentist who loved her deeply. She laughed and said: "This is where my real life begins." I saw her bloom like a flower, walking with sparkling eyes, her future wide open before her.

And then... the war came.

During the first days of the war, we spoke daily, checking on each other. When talk of evacuations began, Aya moved with her family and relatives to her fiancé's house in Nuseirat, which was considered safer and farther from the strikes. About 30 or 40 people were there, Aya's family, her fiancé's family, and displaced relatives.

Not long after...

Their house was bombed.

No one survived except her fiancé.

They all perished.

Aya, who dreamed, planned, and loved life... was gone.

All they found of her was her hand.

Her hand...

The hand that wrote code, the hand that sketched dreams of the future in her notebooks, only her hand remained.

I couldn't comprehend it. When I heard the news, the world turned black. How could this happen? How could Aya, who just days ago sent me updates about our graduation project, vanish so suddenly, so brutally? That night, I didn't sleep. I sat remembering every moment we spent together, every laugh, every tear. I recalled the day we succeeded in our second-year project, when she said: "Dana, I'm proud of us." She was always proud of those around her, seeing beauty in everyone, even when circumstances were tough.

Aya deserved to live. She deserved to wear her graduation gown, see her name displayed in the hall, start her career, and build a warm home with her laughter and intellect.

But what happened... killed even her dreams.

Aya became a story we tell, a pain we carry in our hearts.

But by Allah, we will never forget her.

May Allah have mercy on you, Aya...

You were a star, and you continue to light up our skies, even though you're no longer with us.

Documented by Dana Abu Al-Khair, friend of the martyr Aya

Date of Writing the Story: 2025/06/01

Sajida Yasser Al-Muqaied

Age: 30 years

Original Place: Jabalia

Sajida was a young, ambitious woman who worked as a voice-over artist from home to support her sick daughter, whom she accompanied everywhere, from one hospital to another. Despite her exhaustion, she remained resilient, holding on no matter what.

When the war broke out, we were forced to leave our homes and flee to Nuseirat. The conditions of displacement were incredibly harsh, cramped tents, biting winter cold, and scorching summer heat. Everyone was overwhelmed and exhausted. Sajida bore it all, protecting her daughter and instilling hope in her amidst so much destruction.

But fate showed no mercy. One day, their home in Nuseirat was targeted by heavy artillery shelling. It was a moment of sheer terror and devastation, and they couldn't escape. Sajida, her husband, daughter, and family members were martyred there. We mourned them deeply, as if they had vanished from the entire world.

Her strength continues to inspire us despite her absence. Her loss left an unhealing wound, and every time I think of her, I remember the courage and resilience of Gaza's women, who never surrendered despite oppression and destruction.

These are stories of endurance and determination, of Gazan women who refused to give up, remaining forever in our hearts and memories. We continue to honor their legacy through love and remembrance.

Documented Dana Abu Al-Khair, friend of the martyr Ayah

Date of Writing the Story: 2025/06/01

Fatima

Original Place: Gaza

I am Fatima, a mother, grandmother, and caregiver. Every day in this land feels like an entire lifetime. Since the day I became aware of life, I've heard about wars, pain, and loss. But the October 2023 war was unlike any other, it felt like a dark cloud descending upon us, blotting out the sun, joy, and safety.

I'm not young anymore, and I carry wisdom that suffices for myself and others. Yet, what happened made me feel like a frightened child, unsure where to go. On October 7th, a Saturday morning, I was sitting drinking my coffee, reading the Quran for solace, when suddenly explosions shook the neighborhood. At first, I thought it might be drills, just like every other time, but no, this time was different.

My daughters ran to me, and my little granddaughter clung to my leg, crying: "Grandma, where should we go?" With all the strength I'd accumulated over the years, I wiped her tears and said: "We'll go to Allah." But deep inside, I was terrified.

The first week we spent at my daughter's house in Nuseirat. Three families crammed under one roof, elders and children alike, all surrounded by fear. The sound of planes never left us, and every minute brought a new explosion. Each time, we prayed: "Oh Allah, please don't let anyone close to us be harmed."

After a few days, we received the evacuation order: "Clear the area." What do we leave behind? What do we take with us? We packed a bag with some clothes, diabetes and blood pressure medications, and olive oil from my grandfather's house. My heart ached as I left my home, the one I built brick by brick, with years of sweat, cherishing every corner of it.

We headed to Rafah, and those who have seen Rafah during wartime know the true meaning of hardship. Tents filled with sorrow lined the landscape. The sun burned fiercely, the water was salty, and the nights echoed with barking dogs and the cries of suffering children.

One night in Rafah, my youngest granddaughter coughed violently throughout the night. We tried to warm her, cover her, and give her medicine, but her fever soared. The hospital was far, and the streets were pitch black. I held her close, reciting verses of the Quran while silently crying: "Oh Allah, don't take her away; let her experience happiness just once." Thank Allah, she survived the night and woke up smiling at me the next morning. My heart swelled with relief.

But not everyone we knew survived. We lost our neighbor, Umm Mohammad, who died in an airstrike while preparing dinner for her grandchildren. And we lost Abu Ahmed, who went out to buy bread and returned wrapped in a white shroud.

Between fear and exhaustion, months passed. For five months, we lived between tents and buckets, struggling to find water and medicine. Our dignity bled each time I stood in line for aid, clutching my old ID card.

We returned to Nuseirat, trying to rebuild and start anew, but the new reality proved harder than before. Electricity cuts persisted, gas was unavailable, water supplies dwindled, and life grew increasingly unbearable. When we finally returned to our house, or what used to be our house, we found it stripped bare, without doors, windows, or furniture. Still, I said: "Thank Allah, at least there are walls to protect us."

Today, as I sit in this corner of the house watching the sun set, I tell myself: "We're still standing, and we haven't been defeated, despite everything." This war taught me a lot, it taught me real patience, not the kind written in books, but the kind you live through, endure, and rise from as though unbroken.

I share my story not to complain, but so that those who come after me will know that if they fall, others have fallen and risen again. Life is cruel, but Allah is gentler than its cruelty. Today, I say: "Oh Allah, mend our brokenness, and make this land laugh again, embrace us instead of bidding us farewell."

Date of Writing the Story: 2025/06/01

Maryam Atiyah Helles

Place of Displacement: Barcelona Park

Since leaving our home, I no longer know the feeling of stability. We lived in a small house, but it was our world. There, we laughed, cried, and I cooked simple yet warm meals for my children. Today, I live with my five children in a tent, and everything inside is cold, even the air.

The morning begins with the sound of wind hitting the edges of the tent, followed by the cries of one of my children because they are hungry or sick. Nothing in my day is constant except this relentless anxiety. Sometimes, I stand outside the tent and gaze at the surroundings. This park used to be bustling with people during holidays... now it's filled with tents, tears, and silence.

My children often ask me: "Mom, will there be breakfast today"?

I smile and respond: "Of course, just wait a little longer."

Then I return to the tent, searching through bags for anything, anything at all, to quiet their hunger.

At night, I can't sleep, not because the ground is hard, but because my worries weigh heavier than sleep itself. I hear their breathing around me and wonder how to protect them, how to reassure their hearts when I myself am afraid of tomorrow.

Yet, despite all this, I cling to something small within me... hope. Hope that one day my children will return to school, that I'll cook for them again, and hear their laughter without fear.

My name is Maryam, just a mother trying to embrace life amidst the rubble.

Date of Writing the Story: 2025/06/03

Asmaa

Age: 32 years

Every day, I put on my white coat as if wearing an imaginary shield to protect me from the chaos around me. I thought I had grown accustomed to pain, having worked in the maternity ward for years. I've seen mothers' tears, heard the first cries of newborns, and supported women during their toughest moments. But this war shattered something inside me.

I've been divorced for two years, and my only son, Kareem, lives with his father. I rarely see him, but I keep his picture in my pocket, pulling it out whenever the war intensifies, imagining him safe in my arms. With every explosion, the first thing that comes to mind is his face: Is he okay? Is he as scared as I am?

A few days ago, a pregnant woman in her ninth month arrived at the hospital, abandoned at the doorstep, covered in dust, her wide eyes like the sea, yet silent. We later discovered she had lost her husband, mother, and brother in the bombing, and had no one left.

She entered the delivery room in shock, neither screaming nor asking for anything, just staring at the ceiling. I held her hand and whispered: "I'm here. You're not alone."

I cried with her as we prepared for the birth. There wasn't enough electricity, so we lit the room with phone flashlights and began working.

The baby came into the world crying loudly, as if screaming at life itself. I placed him in her arms, but she didn't move. She kept looking at him, then at me, and asked: "Why did he come now? He should've come before the war"…

In that moment, I felt an unbearable weight. I wished I could turn back time, restore peace to her eyes.

I am Asmaa, working amidst screams and ruins, welcoming new life in a time of death, and trying to convince myself that none of this is in vain.

Date of Writing the Story: 2025/06/01

Story (149)

Hanan

Age: 36 years

Original Place: KhanYounis

I am Layla, a friend of Hanan for over five years. I met her at the beginning of the crisis, and that moment marked the start of a long journey of giving and sacrifice.

Hanan wasn't just a volunteer, she was a vibrant spirit that pulsed with life amidst the ruins. She would reach the camps and displaced people before any organization could; she always led the way with her quick steps and unwavering smile, even as smoke and destruction surrounded her.

Every morning, I'd see her packing her small bag with some medicine, food supplies, and sometimes toys for the children. She would say to me: "Layla, no one is coming to help them. We must be their hope."

On one of the days of intense shelling, Hanan was distributing food at a camp for displaced people near our home. The air was suffocating, and the bombardment relentless. Yet, nothing frightened her. She held every child in her arms, whispering to them that everything would be okay, even though all our hearts were trembling with fear.

Suddenly, we heard the deafening sound of an explosion. A shell had landed close by. We rushed toward Hanan and found her under the rubble, but what amazed me was that she was trying with all her might to lift a small child to help him stand. She didn't leave him alone. Those were her final moments in this world, thinking of others until the very end.

Hanan passed away, but she left behind a legacy of love and compassion. From her, I learned that giving doesn't stop at fear, and that a big heart can shine even in the darkest moments.

Whenever I see a child playing or a smile lighting up someone's face, I remember Hanan... and feel that her spirit is still with us, guarding us, teaching us how to remain human in the midst of these wars.

Documented Layla, friend and neighbor of the martyr Hanan

Date of Writing the Story: 2025/06/03

Nada

Age: 33 years

Nada... The Flower of Education That Spread Its Light in the Heart of Gaza

Nada wasn't just a teacher; she was the soul that moved everything in the school. She loved her students with all her heart, dreaming of being a sun that would light their path through the darkness.

Nada was a young woman in her early thirties, simple in her lifestyle, yet grand in her dreams. She graduated from university with honors and believed that education was the only key that could free our children from the hell of war and occupation.

Every day, she woke up before dawn, preparing her lessons meticulously. She loved seeing the hope in her students' eyes despite all the pain around us.

On the day of the last bombardment, the attack didn't target the school but Nada's home. She had returned home after a long day at work, seeking some rest amid the chaos. But she didn't know it would be her final return.

The bombing struck suddenly on the neighborhood where she lived. Windows shattered, and part of the house collapsed. There was no time to escape or seek help.

There was no formal funeral, the situation was too dangerous. News of her martyrdom spread, leaving deep sorrow and tears in its wake.

I had spoken to her just hours before the bombing. She was telling me about her dreams for this year and the next, sharing her plans to organize new educational activities for the students. I couldn't believe that this conversation would be our final goodbye.

Nada didn't die on the battlefield, but she left an indelible mark on the hearts of everyone who knew her. She was a flower that bloomed in the land of wounds, and her light continues to shine for us despite everything.

I keep her memory alive in my heart, and I recount her story so we never forget her. Her spirit remains with us, reminding us that hope must endure even in the hardest of days.

Nada didn't just sacrifice her body; her soul lives on, hovering over the schools of Gaza, inspiring every teacher and student to continue the journey, to live life despite all the pain.

Documented by A Friend of the Martyr Nada

Date of Writing the Story: 2025/06/01

Umm Noor

"Umm Noor... The Fire of War and the Patience of a Mother"

My name is Umm Noor; I am 35 years old and live in the Gaza Strip, in a neighborhood where houses once stood closely together like the hearts of its residents, before the war tore them apart. I am a divorced woman, separated for five years, raising my three children alone: Noor (12 years old), Hamza (9 years old), and little Maryam, who is not yet four.

Since my separation, I chose not to be a victim. I worked cleaning houses in the mornings, and sometimes I sewed on a used sewing machine gifted to me by a kind neighbor. The road wasn't easy, but I always told myself: "If I'm not both a mother and father to them, then who will be"?

When the latest war began, I was in the kitchen preparing a modest lunch when the entire house shook. The sound of the explosion was so close that Maryam screamed and fell into my arms, crying. In that moment, I thought of only one thing: How do I protect my children?

We fled our home to the nearby school, like hundreds of other families. We took nothing with us but a blanket, some dry bread, and a small picture of my late father.

In the classroom where we gathered, eyes were lost, and hearts were terrified, but I didn't show my fear. I held my children close, as if embracing my own heart, telling them simple stories and singing lullabies to Maryam so she could sleep, even as the sounds of shelling shook the walls.

On the first night in the school, I didn't sleep a wink. Maryam moaned from the cold, Noor cried silently, and Hamza trembled beside me. I took off my cloak and covered them with it, sitting through the night reciting prayers and wondering... would the morning ever come?

I wasn't a hero in anyone's eyes. I was just a mother doing the impossible to keep my children alive. One night, our house was bombed, it was completely destroyed. I didn't even have tears left. I looked at Hamza and said: "The house means nothing as long as we're together."

The children grew hungrier by the day. One day, all I had left was a little flour. I mixed it with water and lit a fire with wood in the schoolyard. I baked small loaves of bread, dividing each loaf into three pieces while I remained hungry.

Those moments... they were moments of pure resilience. I resisted hunger, endured with patience, and forced a smile so their young spirits wouldn't collapse.

Weeks passed, and the situation worsened. My hands went numb from the cold, and my back ached from sleeping on the hard ground, but my heart remained strong... because they were with me.

During the war, I learned that a woman isn't just someone who protects her home but someone who protects life itself. I lit fires, warmed my children, mended torn clothes, and taught Noor multiplication tables as she wrote on a torn piece of cardboard.

I'm not extraordinary, I'm just a woman, a mother with nothing but her inner strength. I didn't choose the war, but I chose to resist it in my own way.

I am a divorced woman from Gaza, standing tall in the heart of the storm, not because I don't feel fear, but because I love my children more than my fear.

Date of Writing the Story: 2025/06/01

Maha Al-OmraniAge: 38 years

Original Place: Gaza

Maha... The Voice of Taraweeh That Vanished

I am Maha, born with cerebral palsy and epilepsy. Since childhood, I've been in a wheelchair, but I swear by Allah, I never felt like I was lacking. On the contrary… I always said: "Praise be to Allah who gave me a mind, a heart, and contentment."

Our home is simple, next to the mosque where I used to go every day. I was deeply connected to prayer, especially during Ramadan. I never missed a single Taraweeh prayer. The girls in the neighborhood would tell me: "You have the purest soul in the mosque, Maha."

I waited for Ramadan from one year to the next, eager to experience its atmosphere, hear the recitation of the Quran, smell the scent of prayer mats, and pour my heart out in prayer to Allah.

The happiest moments for me were when I heard the call to prayer, and I began preparing myself for prayer, the wheelchair ready, the scarf prepared, and the intention firmly set.

But this past Ramadan, everything changed suddenly because we had barely returned from being displaced in the south, and finally, this Ramadan was supposed to be in Shujaiya.

In the middle of the night, we woke up to the sound of a loud explosion. I felt the window about to fly off its hinges. My sister rushed to me and said: "Maha, the war is back."

I didn't believe her at first. I told her: "Stop joking!" But the sound of the planes made it clear that it was true.

For the first two days, I tried to stay strong. I opened the Quran and said: "My Allah, grant me light in this darkness."

But the shelling grew closer, and the mosque I used to attend… was bombed.

What hurt me most was seeing the rubble where the mosque once stood. Later, I heard that the imam had been martyred, and the mosque was reduced to ruins.

Since that day, I haven't been able to hear the voice of Taraweeh prayers, not from the mosque, nor from recordings. Everything fell silent.

I would sit alone, reading the Quran in a low voice, remembering the imam's voice as he said: "Straighten your rows... Align yourselves... Allah is Great."

Prayer continued, but without the congregation, without the atmosphere, without the joy I once felt.

I kept telling myself: "Maha, the war took the mosque, but it can't take the faith from your heart."

Every day before dawn, I'd wait for a moment of stillness, pray by myself, and speak to Allah:

"You see me, I can't move, but my heart comes to You, and my eyes cry for You."

Everyone around me talked about bread and water, but my pain was greater, I lost the place that made me feel like I was standing just like everyone else, not less than anyone.

But even now, sitting in my wheelchair under the sound of planes, I say:

"As long as the Quran is on my lap, I fear nothing."

I am Maha Al-Omrani. Even if the war silenced the voice of the mosque, my prayers are still rising, and my heart has never stopped.

Date of Writing the Story: 2025/06/01

Mai

Age: 34 years

"In the Embrace of the Quran Amidst the Fire of War"

A mother of three children, divorced for five years. After my divorce, I've been raising my kids alone. I try to be both a mother and a father at the same time, despite all the exhaustion and responsibility.

After the birth of my youngest daughter, "Maryam," I suffered complications, including severe back pain. Doctors told me it was due to the delivery… and since then, I've been confined to a wheelchair. It's hard for me to walk; even going to the bathroom requires help.

Despite all this, I always tried to live my life as normally as possible. During Ramadan, I would gather my children around me. We prayed together and read the Quran. I found peace when I read, and I forgot the pain in my back.

On Saturday, October 7th, we were asleep when suddenly we heard the sound of powerful explosions early in the morning. I woke up terrified, and my daughters started crying. We didn't understand what was happening, but the TV came on and announced: "The aggression on Gaza has begun."

I tried to calm the girls down and said: "Don't be afraid, we'll stay together."

I started gathering a few things, my small Quran, some clothes, and packed them into a backpack, preparing in case we had to leave and flee.

Days passed, and every day the shelling got closer. Water was cut off. Electricity went out; food was scarce… but I held onto the Quran, reading it every day aloud. My daughters would sit beside me, and we'd read together, repeating:

"Allah is sufficient for us, and He is the best protector."

The nights were difficult. I would recite the Quran from memory, especially Surah Al-Baqarah and Yaseen. When I felt fear, I would quietly recite the supplication for distress and hold Maryam close to my chest.

The hardest day was when the glass shattered from our windows due to a nearby bombing. Maryam was sleeping next to me, and by Allah's grace, she wasn't hit. I wiped her blood with my scarf and thanked Allah that it was only a minor injury.

No one came to check on us, no organizations, no aid. Our food became dry bread and tomatoes, and when the gas ran out, we cooked over wood fires.

I told my daughters: "Every bite we eat is resilience in the face of the occupation."

I couldn't flee or evacuate; moving on my wheelchair over the rubble was impossible. I said: "I'll stay in my house; death will come to us sooner or later."

People would ask: "Why didn't you flee to the south?" And I would reply: "I'm not alone; I have my children and my faith."

The war ended above ground, but its scars linger within us. The electricity is still cut off, food is hard to come by, and the wheelchair pains me more than ever.

But to this day, I haven't let a single day pass without holding the Quran and saying: "Praise be to Allah, who granted me patience and faith."

Date of Writing the Story: 2025/06/01

Umm Rami

Umm Rami lived in Shujaiya, a mother of five children, the eldest of whom was Rami, after whom she was named. Her husband passed away seven years ago from a stroke, leaving her with a heavy burden, but she never complained. She worked in a bakery, cleaning and packing bread. She'd return home to cook, teach her children, wash clothes, pray, and make supplications. Everyone who knew her would say:

"This woman is a mountain; no wind can shake her."

Before the war, Umm Rami was happy. Her son Rami had finished high school with excellent grades and wanted to study engineering. Her eldest daughter planned to start nursing school. They had hope, a bit of stability amidst the chaos, despite poverty, despite frequent power cuts, and despite the suffocating blockade.

But on October 7, 2023, everything changed.

Missiles rained down like thunder, their sound terrifying hearts. Umm Rami was at the bakery when she heard people screaming: "War! War!" Barefoot, she ran across the street under the bombardment, returned home, gathered her children, packed a few clothes into a bag, and fled without thinking, just a mother desperate to protect.

She went to her sister's house in Deir al-Balah, but there was no room. Then they moved to a school in Nuseirat, and when a nearby school was bombed, she took her children and fled to a tent in Tel al-Sultan, where the cold was merciless.

In the tent, Umm Rami experienced the suffering she had only heard about in the news. She drank salty water, cooked over a wood fire, and placed bread under the mat to keep it safe from rats.

Her youngest daughter fell ill, and she searched among the people for medicine but found none. She begged pharmacies: "Just something to lower the fever… the child is trembling."

One day, a missile struck a nearby tent. Umm Rami jumped on top of her children, hugging them tightly, her body becoming a shield. Later, when asked: "Were you afraid?"

She replied:

"I don't fear for myself; I fear losing one of them."

Days passed, and the cold turned to heat, the dust to sweat, and the cold returned again. Rami helped her carry bread from the queue and fetch water, but one day, when the queue was bombed, Rami, her eldest son, her support, and the joy of her life, was killed.

Umm Rami walked to the sea and spoke to the waves:

"You took him… but I'm still standing."

She buried him with a handful of dirt, without a shroud, without a farewell. She wiped her tears and returned to the tent, shouting to her children:

"No one will be lost as long as I'm alive."

After two months in the tent, orders came to evacuate the area. She carried the remnants of her life and moved again, to another place, then another, and then another… each time rebuilding. She would lay a mat on the ground, put up a tarp, and tell her daughters:

"Clean up, let the place smell nice."

And she never slept. The night became her companion in tears, and the morning brought endless work. She ate a bite, giving the rest to her youngest. She mended pants with a needle and thread, boiled water heated by the sun so her daughters could bathe, taught them, and instilled hope despite the pain.

When she returned to her home in Shujaiya, she found only a broken wall, dust, and the smell of gunpowder. She stood, hugged the wall, and said:

"We're back, oh home… we're the ones who remained."

Her eldest daughter entered nursing school despite the bombings and told her mother:

"I want to heal people like you healed us, you planted hope in us despite our wounds."

In her final days, Umm Rami suffered in silence. She didn't complain, but her body was slowly breaking down. Fatigue, oppression, displacement, hunger, the loss of Rami, the cold, and the fear, all left their marks on her soul before her body.

She would tell her eldest daughter:

"I'm fine, my dear, just my body is tired a little."

But the truth was, she was dying inside. She breathed with difficulty, and her heart bled, not from illness, but from carrying so much sorrow.

On a rainy night, the tent shook from the wind, rain poured in from every direction, and the cold bit through to the bone. Umm Rami rose in the middle of the night, covered her children with her jacket, sat on the ground, raised her hands to the sky, and said:

"Oh Allah, take me if my death brings relief... but keep my children safe."

The next day, she didn't wake up.

Her daughter found her sitting on the ground, her head tilted, her eyes closed, and a rosary in her hand. No one heard her moan, no one heard her farewell, but the heavens surely did.

Umm Rami died, but her story lives on.

Date of Writing the Story: 2025/06/01

Umm Hatem

Original Place: Shujaiya

I am Umm Hatem from Gaza, a mother of seven children whom I raised with my heart and soul, dreaming of rejoicing in their growth and seeing them build their homeland.

But Allah's will is what He chooses to do, four of my children were martyred in past wars, and each time, I was torn apart by an indescribable pain.

The new war was not easy on us. My youngest son, Alaa, was still with us, a strong young man, active in the neighborhood. But one day, during a sudden bombardment, Alaa was martyred… It was a moment beyond words; my heart stopped beating.

My husband, despite his illness and old age, carried Alaa's body to the hospital with his own hands, trying to stop the bleeding from my precious boy.

Not long after, Allah took him too, he couldn't bear losing his children, especially Alaa. He left me alone with seven children, carrying a pain that never fades.

The house is now filled with silence, and pictures of my martyred children hang on the walls, reminding me of their loss every moment.

Every day, I pray and ask Allah for patience, saying: "Oh Allah, be with me because my heart can't bear this pain."

Despite all the suffering, I am Umm Hatem, I stood firm against every storm, raised my remaining children, and tried to instill hope in them despite the destruction.

The war didn't break me, but it taught me how to be strong and continue walking despite the wounds.

I'm not just the mother of martyrs, I am a symbol of patience and hope for every mother living through the same story.

Date of Writing the Story: 2025/06/01

Baraa Al-Omrani

Age: 25 years

Original Place: Shujaiya

I am Baraa Al-Omrani, a daughter of Gaza and a mother of twin girls. My eyes never leave them, not even for a minute. My husband is a good man, but life has become difficult, and it's hard for us to provide even the simplest things for our children. The girls are now one and a half years old, and my heart breaks when I see them cry from hunger or exhaustion.

From the start of the war, our lives changed. The small amounts of food that used to reach us became scarcer, and prices skyrocketed. Before my pregnancy, I worked a simple job to support my family, but after Allah blessed me with twin girls, I had to quit. I left work to dedicate myself to them, but the responsibility grew heavier, and so did the worries.

The lack of food didn't just affect my health, it also affected my milk supply. Sometimes I feel my milk running low, and anxiety never leaves me. Once, I tried to buy formula, but the prices were unimaginable, and even when I found some, it wasn't enough for everyone. What pains me most is seeing the girls suffer, crying, restless, and unable to find comfort, and I can't soothe them.

We fled our home in the north when the shelling became intense. Our tent is small, the cold penetrates deep, and water is scarce. We have to ration our food carefully, sometimes reducing portions so it lasts for everyone.

Everyone around me is suffering, women like me, mothers of boys and girls, enduring the same pain. At times, I feel my heart might shatter, but I remind myself: "I must be patient, for these girls, I must be strong."

My husband does his best to provide, though he struggles. He tries to find any work, no matter how small. Together, we support each other and lift each other's spirits. Despite everything, there's still hope.

Hope that one day peace will return to Gaza, and we'll be able to provide every child with enough food, warm milk, and a normal life.

I am the voice of every mother exhausted by hunger and pain, every mother who dreams of seeing her children grow up safely, peacefully, and with dignity.

Date of Writing the Story: 2025/06/01

Umm Sameer

Age: 44 years

I am Umm Sameer, from Gaza, with five young children, the oldest is ten, and the youngest is still very small. My entire life revolved around them: cooking for them, taking care of them, and dreaming of a day when there would be safety and peace.

But suddenly, the war began, and I was sleeping with my little ones. We woke up to the sound of shelling and explosions that shook our house and the whole neighborhood.

I quickly gathered my children, thinking about how to feed them amidst all this destruction.

Electricity was cut off, water was irregular, and there was no gas. I had to cook over firewood, resources were scarce, and the bread we had was almost stale.

Every day, my children would ask:"Mom, is there food?"And every day, my heart broke as I could only offer them a piece of bread or a little lentil stew.

I'd go out to collect broken wood from the neighborhood, and my children, even the youngest, would come with me to help light the fire.

Cooking was the hardest part, the fire was small, and the food was scarce, but I had to smile and cheer them up so they wouldn't feel the pain of hunger.

Once, my youngest daughter cried from hunger, and all I had was a dry piece of bread and a splash of oil. I dipped the bread in oil and gave it to her, saying:
"Be patient, my love, tomorrow will be better."

Despite all these challenges, I sit and pray, asking Allah to give me strength and protect my children. When the shelling gets close, we run and gather together, and I try to stay strong for them.

I am Umm Sameer, and life has taught me patience and resilience. I face everything for my children, giving them hope to live for.

Date of Writing the Story: 2025/06/01

Nuha Bakroun

Age: 35 years Original Place: Shujaiya

I am Nuha Bakroun, a wife and mother from Gaza. Before the last war, we lived in our house in the south, and everything was normal. But when the war began, we were forced to flee and live in a tent set up in front of the ruins of our completely destroyed home.

Ramadan came in the midst of the war, and I tried my best to prepare my children, fast, and pray despite all the hardship. We lived in the small tent amidst the rubble, facing many difficulties, but we endured.

After Ramadan ended, we were ordered to leave our area and abandon the tent for another place farther from danger. I went on a journey with my family, we were tired, hungry, and scared of the unknown.

When I returned from the trip, I suddenly heard that our tent had been burned by a shell. My heart stopped! Thank Allah I was outside the tent at the time, or I wouldn't be alive today.

I lost the house I spent years building and the tent that held all the hope and warmth for my family, but Allah saved me and made me stand strong despite the pain.

I am Nuha, and my heart is full of sorrow, but nothing can break my will because my family needs me, and I must be strong and patient, even if the whole world is against us.

After leaving the tent, which was burned by the shell, life became even harder. We moved from place to place, trying to find shelter to protect us from the cold and hunger.

I'd wake up in the morning and try to organize my children, the eldest took on responsibility to help me and ease my burden a little.

Food became almost nonexistent. I prepared dry bread or leftover rice for them, and every day I prayed to Allah to provide us with sustenance to fill my children's stomachs.

We sat under a tree or in a nearby house belonging to people who hadn't yet fled, talking about losses and the fear of tomorrow.

There were many moments when I felt deeply alone, but I knew I had to stand strong for my children, even if my heart was breaking.

At night, when everyone was silent, I prayed, cried, and asked Allah for victory and patience. Sometimes, I told my children stories about Gaza before the war so they wouldn't forget their roots or lose hope.

Despite all the destruction, hunger, and fear, I remain steadfast, trying to build new hope for my children, even if the whole world is against us.

Date of Writing the Story: 2025/06/01

Umm Rima

Age: 36 years

Original Place: Gaza

I am Umm Rima, living in Gaza, and a mother of four children. The war came suddenly, destroying everything around me. Half of our house collapsed, food became scarce, and income disappeared.

Every day, I wake up wondering how to provide a meal for my children, but there's no easy solution in wartime.

Bread prices soared, food supplies vanished, and I struggle with my children's hunger, they look at me with pleading eyes. My heart breaks as I try to hide my exhaustion and smile so they don't feel afraid.

Each day, we collect small cans of food from here and there, from charities, neighbors, and kind-hearted people who understand our suffering.

I cook over a small fire, doing what I can, even if the food is simple, it must exist.

Hunger isn't just pain in the stomach; it's also pain in the heart, but I won't let it break me.

Date of Writing the Story: 2025/06/01

Reem Jeninah

Age: 36 years

Original Place: Sheikh Radwan

I am Reem, a woman from Gaza, married to an older man, but we have no children. My life was peaceful until the war turned everything upside down.

One morning during the war, we were sleeping in our house when suddenly the shelling intensified around us. Our decades-old house collapsed under a pile of rubble. I felt the world crumbling around me, the sound of stones closing in, and everything went dark.

I told myself: "I must stay strong; I must get out from under the rubble." With great effort, my husband and I managed to move bit by bit. After three long hours of fear and darkness, we emerged from the rubble. We were exhausted, my body ached, and my fears grew, but thank Allah, we survived.

There was no time to think much because we had no home to return to. We were forced to flee to a tent in the south, a very small tent, but it was the only refuge we had. The weather was cold, food was scarce, and electricity had been cut off for days.

The south was different, many displaced people had gathered there, all living in the same state of fear, hunger, and sadness. I tried to help my husband despite our exhaustion and organized our daily lives, even if they were simple. Each day brought a new challenge.

I went out to collect bread or search for food from aid organizations, and each time, the weight of fatigue grew heavier on my shoulders. Sometimes, alone in the tent, I'd hear the voices of children forced to grow up too quickly because of the war, and I'd feel immense internal pain.

After weeks, when things calmed down slightly, we decided to return to our second home in Sheikh Radwan. The house was damaged, the walls disfigured, and the furniture reduced to ashes. But it was our home, and hope still lingered.

Life had been simple and beautiful once. I moved between the neighborhood and neighbors, trying to help people and see hope despite the destruction. Sometimes, I'd sit with my husband, talking about the future, about the tomorrow that must come, no matter how difficult.

Though I have no children, my heart is big enough to carry the burdens of the neighborhood and the neighbors who lost everything. I participated in distributing aid and supported people with kind words or small acts of assistance.

I stood firm against the war, displacement, and destruction. Every day, I live with new hope, despite all the pain. The war didn't break me; instead, it taught me patience, strength, and the value of life that cannot be replaced.

Date of Writing the Story: 2025/06/01

Sabah

Age: 21 years

Original Place: Sheikh Radwan

I am Sabah, a student at Al-Azhar University studying pharmacy. My life wasn't easy, but I never gave up and decided to continue my journey despite all the difficult circumstances.

The war destroyed our home, forcing us to flee and live in a small tent in the south. The tent was cramped, unbearably cold in winter and scorching in summer, but it was the only place where we felt safe.

I would wake up early in the morning, preparing myself for study, even when there was no electricity or stable internet. I studied by the light of candles and sometimes by the dim glow of my phone, my heart full of hope.

The biggest challenge came during exam times, when I had to study for long hours amidst the sounds of shelling and people around me preoccupied with survival rather than education.

I tried to find a quiet corner in the tent, opening my books and focusing on my lessons. Sometimes the books would get wet from the rain or dirty, but I didn't let anything stop me.

Occasionally, I organized small study groups with other girls in the tent to support and encourage one another.

I always told myself: "I'm not just studying pharmacy; I'm studying to help my family and my country one day."

After the war ended, we returned to our home, and I had the chance to attend university lectures more regularly. But my heart remained with all the girls still struggling under the same conditions.

My dreams are big, and my hope in Allah is immense. Despite everything, I will never stop studying or striving to build a better future.

Date of Writing the Story: 2025/06/01

Nisreen

I am Nisreen, a daughter of Gaza, suffering from a chronic liver disease for years. My life was already difficult, but the war made things much worse.

Liver disease requires special care, especially clean food and water. But during the war, there was no clean water or electricity to help me maintain my health.

The water we drank was often contaminated, worsening my condition. At times, I became extremely weak and unable to move.

The war made everything harder, hospitals were overwhelmed and unable to provide proper treatment. As conditions deteriorated, so did my health.

I tried to take care of myself, washing my hands even when water was scarce, but sometimes it wasn't enough. I feared contamination and the progression of my illness.

At night, when the electricity went out, I tried to rest and protect myself, but thoughts of my illness and the lack of clean water haunted me.

I dream of a day when there will be clean water, safe hospitals, and a better life.

Date of Writing the Story: 2025/06/01

Shahed Muneer Salem

Age: 15 years

Shahed... A Flower Plucked Before It Could Bloom

In the springtime of her life, Shahed Muneer Salem, at just 15 years old, was writing the first chapter of her dream. She was a quiet girl, carrying in her heart a warmth that could comfort a troubled world. Shahed was beloved by everyone, she brought warmth to those around her and stood by her friends in every moment, like a little soldier in the battle of life.

Shahed wasn't just a 15-year-old girl; she was a dream sketched in school notebooks, a smile that adorned moments of displacement and war, and a whisper to the future: "We will survive and achieve everything we've dreamed of."

But war, as always, pays no heed to dreams.

Her friend wrote a heartbreaking message to our platform:

"Shahed was so kind and loving, always calm and gentle. My dear friend, you left too soon, with dreams yet to fulfill. We used to plan our future together, but I never imagined you'd leave without us. I miss you so much."

In an instant, Shahed was taken from us, as if the sky hurried her departure. She was martyred just days before her last conversation with her friend, when she said:

"Take care of yourself, and greet your mom and Aseel for me. I love you."

It was as if she was saying goodbye, her heart knowing that parting was near and departure closer than we imagined.

She dreamed of becoming a martyr, often repeating this to her friend. And she departed as she wished, a martyr in a land that knows no peace.

But those left behind died while still alive. Her friend said:

"I feel like I'm dying while living... The memories kill me a hundred times over."

240

Shahed is gone, but her warmth still colors the walls of tents, school notebooks, and nighttime conversations among friends. The story remains incomplete without her.

May Allah have mercy on you, Shahed. You were a small flower plucked by war before it could bloom, but your fragrance will remain with us forever.

Documented by Shahed's Friend

Date of Writing the Story: 2025/06/01

Aliah Rami Al-Hanawi

Age: 35 years

Profession: Doctor

Aliah... The Doctor Who Healed Others' Wounds and Departed in Silence

In a time when safety was scarce and amid the smoke of death and rubble, Aliah was an unextinguished flame of light. With a radiant face and an ever-present smile, she carried warmth in her heart that couldn't be measured, and strength that comforted the weak.

Aliah was 35 years old, a mother of four children, a loving wife, and a doctor at Al-Shifa Hospital. She saved lives and eased pain during the hardest moments of the war. She never faltered, comforting her colleagues and reminding them that some families had lost everything, and that it was their duty to remain standing for them.

One day, she told her younger sister: "There are families erased entirely from civil records... We must be there for them."

Little did she know that her name, along with her husband's and children's, would also be erased from that record.

Her younger sister wrote to our platform, battling grief and disbelief:

"Aliah, her husband, and their four children were martyred after their home was targeted... She was so kind and loving, my pillar of support. She always encouraged me and had dreams and achievements she wanted to fulfill, but she left too soon."

Aliah was a mother, a refuge, a friend, and a sister, a support to all who knew her, planting hope in every heart. But she left, taking with her an entire household and countless dreams that never saw the light of day.

Yet memory does not forget, and hearts do not extinguish. Aliah remains a pure legacy, a fragrant memory, and an eternal remembrance.

She left behind beautiful memories and a good impact on everyone. May Allah have mercy on them and grant us paradise as our meeting place, Allah willing.

Documented by Her Younger Sister

Date of Writing the Story: 2025/06/01

Rahaf Al-Haddad

Age: 14 years

Rahaf... The Purity of Heart and the Final White Garment

At the age of blossoming youth, Rahaf Al-Haddad, aged 14, carried a heart larger than her years and light that overflowed from her small eyes. She was a child, yes, but she thought as adults rarely do, spoke with confidence, and planned her final journey without telling us she wouldn't return.

That day, their home was crowded with displaced people, like many houses in Gaza that groaned under the weight of their inhabitants and their pain. Amid the chaos, Rahaf wore a white blouse. Her mother looked at her and gently said, tinged with worry:

"Why are you wearing white? It'll get dirty..."

But Rahaf, with a calm smile, replied with a confidence possessed only by the pure-hearted:

"So I can go to Allah tidy and clean."

She also told her father, as if aware that fate was approaching with heavy steps:

"If I become a martyr, I'll intercede for seventy people, and all of you will enter paradise."

On that very day, October 25, 2023, she achieved her wish, departing to her Allah in her white garment and pure heart, leaving behind indescribable pain and a testament of love and salvation.

Her sister wrote to our platform words that war could not steal:

"She was a different child, as if she knew... Rahaf left clean, her face smiling. She was an angel, and now she has returned to Allah."

Rahaf is gone, but her story remains, a purity that will outshine the darkness of these times, and a memory that will bear witness to a generation that lived death in the size of childhood.

Date of Writing the Story: 2025/06/01

Nihaya Abdullah Talat Al-Wahidi

Age: 13 years

Nihaya... A Flower That Didn't Finish Her Exam

Nihaya was born on June 2, 2012, the firstborn of a loving father and mother, and the older sister to three younger siblings. She carried in her heart a tenderness beyond her years and a warmth that overflowed onto those around her.

In the midst of war, Nihaya chose to color the ashes. She spent her time crafting handmade items, embroidering, and beading, holding the thread and needle as if stitching another story of life. She loved children, played with them, and taught them, her dream of becoming a teacher emerging from a mature spirit racing ahead of her age.

After their displacement, Nihaya longed for her school and dreamed of the war ending so she could return to her classroom. When a temporary school was set up in Deir al-Balah, she enrolled. There, despite pain and exhaustion, she excelled, and everyone, teachers, the principal, and classmates, loved her.

One day, after taking her Arabic exam for the sixth grade, she happily told her   mother:
"I'm sure I got a perfect score!"

The next day, she was supposed to take her Islamic Education exam, which required memorizing Surah Ar-Rahman. She mastered the surah by sunset, played with her younger siblings, and went to bed early to wake up refreshed for the exam...

But war, as always, betrayed every beautiful moment.

After dinner, shelling struck near their tent. Shrapnel hit Nihaya in the neck and above her eye... She remained asleep and never woke up. Her family was injured, but Nihaya was the only one who left without saying goodbye.

Her dreams carried her to heaven.

Nihaya passed away while memorizing Surah Ar-Rahman, leaving behind unfulfilled dreams, wounded hearts, and a pure memory that will never fade.

Nihaya didn't finish her exam, but she succeeded in kindness and virtue, leaving a pain mixed with pride in our hearts.

Documented Her Sister

Date of Writing the Story: 2025/06/01

Aisha Ahmad Qasem

Age: 27 years

Aisha... A Mother Without Children, Yet Many Hearts Called Her "Mom"

At 27, Aisha was a vibrant young woman overflowing with affection and warmth. After marrying, she continued her education with determination, graduating from Al-Quds Open University with a degree in Basic Education, carrying big dreams and a heart full of love for children and teaching.

Unable to find work after graduation, she didn't sit idle. She opened a small center called "Al-Tafawuq" (Excellence), a haven for learning and love. She welcomed children into her home, offering all the knowledge, warmth, and hope she had. Though she had no children of her own, she became a "mother" to countless children who clung to her as if she were their small homeland.

She was loving, humble, and generous, filling her home and surroundings with unique tenderness and a smile as refreshing as a breeze.

On November 6, 2023, Aisha and her husband, Abdul Rahman Al-Shaer, departed together, hand in hand, to what she always believed was the final destination of the good-hearted: paradise.

"Ayoush, my older sister, my second mother, the twin of my soul, my companion on the journey, and keeper of my secrets... She was the gentle, kind, and innocent one, with a big heart and pure laughter during our gatherings. She was generous and giving, wishing goodness for everyone, deeply loving children and her husband... And they both went to paradise together."

Aisha wasn't just a sister, wife, or teacher; she was a small homeland walking on two feet, a safe haven for all who knew her, and a lasting, beautiful legacy.

With her martyrdom, the family lost a pillar, and children lost a kind face that used to explain life to them. But we believe that Aisha, despite her absence, continues to plant light in the hearts of those who loved her.

Date of Writing the Story: 2025/06/01

Razan Muheisen

Original Place: Gaza

Childhood for Razan Muheisen wasn't just about toys and colorful notebooks, it was a world she tried to live in as much as possible before the slow death of war claimed her.

Razan, a child from the Shujaiya neighborhood, was barely six years old. She studied at the "Al-Khayr" kindergarten in Gaza, beloved by everyone, healthy and radiant, with a smile that lit up every corner. But war spares nothing.

Two months after her family fled Gaza to Deir al-Balah, Razan's painful journey began. Her small body slowly withered. Her hair fell out, ulcers appeared on her delicate skin, and chronic symptoms silently consumed her day by day.

In May 2024, she was taken to the American Hospital in Rafah, but the intensifying aggression on the city forced her family to bring her back to Al-Aqsa Hospital. There, she suffered from severe malnutrition, blood clots, and other symptoms doctors couldn't fully explain.

Razan was like a rose, beautiful, soft-spoken, and fond of molokhia and grilled meat. Her dreams were simple: to recover, to return to her kindergarten, to wear a new dress, and to laugh, even if just a little.

Her family tried every way to secure travel permits for her treatment, but the blockade was stronger than their prayers, and the borders narrower than her cries.

On November 7, 2024, Razan passed away, not from a rocket or bombardment, but from the slow poison of war seeping into the bodies of children without noise.

Razan left behind an unrelenting ache and a small face still etched in the memories of all who saw her, smiling and wilting at the same time.

Razan wasn't just a number. She was a whole life… extinguished.

Documented One of the Martyr's Relatives

Date of Writing the Story: 2025/06/01

Duha Jarwan

Age: 29 years

Duha... A Smile That Never Fades

At 29, Duha walked steadily toward a future she had always dreamed of, carrying passion in her heart, brilliant thoughts in her mind, and a unique beauty in her soul that resembled no one else.

She studied English and graduated with distinction, excelling not only academically but also in spirit, kindness, and a smile that never faded, even in the darkest moments.

Duha was a rare blend of calmness and strength. She knew how to embrace people with kind words and build hope amidst destruction. Wherever she went, she changed the atmosphere, turning sorrow into peace. When she was present, pain felt lighter, and when she was absent, a heavy silence settled.

Her dreams weren't ordinary. She envisioned a future filled with giving, education, and service, weaving her aspirations with threads of light until occupation shattered the backbone of her dreams.

On February 21, 2024, Duha was martyred.

She didn't leave behind just tears on the faces of those who loved her but a lasting impact, a picture, a word, a touch, and a beautiful memory that stays with everyone who knew her. She was the embodiment of the conscious Palestinian woman who never stopped dreaming and never compromised her love for life, even amid ruins.

Duha is gone, but no one remembers her without smiling through tears. Her smile was unforgettable.

Documented One of the Martyr's Relatives

Date of Writing the Story: 2025/06/01

Sundus Jamal Shalabi

Sundus… Two Hearts That Stopped Together

Sundus wasn't an ordinary martyr, she was a story of longing and betrayal. To kill the dreams of a woman and her unborn child is a pain history cannot describe.

Sundus was pregnant, dreaming of the moment she would hold him in her arms and sing him the lullaby she had imagined in her mind. She never saw him, and he never saw her.

Before departing, she wrote words to him, a letter to a child she only knew in her heart:

"When you grow up and become a hero, know that your mother loved you from the first moment and waited for you like never before… But the war didn't allow us to meet. Forgive me, my little one."

Sundus didn't leave this life alone. She carried her unborn child, a heart that never saw the light, a small dream swallowed by war without guilt.

Sundus ascended as a martyr, leaving behind a double tragedy, an expectant mother and a child who never even cried his first cry of life.

Documented   One   of   the   Martyr's   Relatives
Date of Writing the Story: 2025/06/01

Iman Al-Shanti

Profession: Journalist

Iman, a brave journalist, wrote to document, to bear witness, and to say what others couldn't. She wasn't just a news carrier but part of the truth, walking through the alleys of destruction, holding her pen as someone might hold a glimmer of hope.

She witnessed massacres, saw devastation, wrote about it, and returned home   to   ask: "How am I still alive? How do I keep writing after all this?"

In a moment of inner exhaustion, she wrote her final words, marveling at her survival after witnessing such annihilation and ruin.

But she didn't finish that day. Hours later, Iman was martyred.

She knew death was near, but it didn't frighten her. She understood that her voice would endure and that the truth she spoke wouldn't be buried.

Iman wasn't just a journalist. She was a living conscience, a voice for the grieving, and a living memory of days that won't be forgotten.

With her martyrdom, a pen fell, but the truth she wrote remains unshaken.

Documented   A   Colleague   of   the   Martyr   Iman
Date of Writing the Story: 2025/06/01

Umm Hamza Al-Tanani

We married in 2023, planning every detail of our small and big lives. Ahmed was the man I always dreamed of, kind-hearted, prayerful, and generous to everyone around him.

We eagerly awaited the birth of our first child, Hamza, with indescribable joy, despite the war surrounding us.

But fate didn't write this dream for us to complete together.

While my son was born in the south, Ahmed was in the north, fighting, enduring every hardship, and trying to stay strong for us.

His only wish was to smell his child, to hold him in his arms, to share the joy of fatherhood... but the war bound him, and harsh conditions prevented him from reaching us.

Then came the moment I never expected, Ahmed was martyred, leaving my heart shattered and my soul torn. He left me alone to face life, raise Hamza without a father, and try to explain to him one day that his father was a hero who loved him more than anything, though he never met him.

The pain of war isn't just in destruction but in loss, broken dreams, and moments that will never return.

Now, I carry a great responsibility, trying to be both mother and father, holding Ahmed's memory in my heart, and telling the story of a love that didn't die, even with departure.

Date of Writing the Story: 2025/06/01

Alaa Al-Hamss

Profession: Journalist

Journalist Alaa Al-Hamss was the voice of truth in the midst of darkness. She worked tirelessly with Al-Masirah TV in Yemen, Sond News Agency, and other media organizations, documenting events with honesty and courage.

Alaa survived an earlier strike on her home, but fate was quicker in the next attack, severely wounding her. She succumbed to her injuries in Rafah, ascending as a martyr.

Alaa was a symbol of determination and strength, despite the losses her family endured, including most of her relatives who were martyred in the same aggression.

Though Alaa is gone, she left an indelible mark in journalism, and her voice continues to resonate in the hearts of all who knew her or heard of her bravery.

Documented A Colleague of the Martyr

Date of Writing the Story: 2025/06/01

Rawan Maher Zagout

Profession: Doctor

Rawan, or as we lovingly called her "Al-Rawana," was not only my cousin but also a light that illuminated our lives. Kind-hearted, humble, and compassionate, she always wore a smile that never left her face. Despite the hardships she endured, she remained ambitious and full of love for life.

She lost her father at a young age, but instead of letting it hold her back, she persevered with determination. She excelled in high school and pursued her dream of becoming a doctor at Al-Azhar University, aspiring to ease others' pain and save lives.

We were eagerly awaiting her graduation, proud of her success, but fate had other plans. Rawan did not leave Jabalia Camp alive, she was martyred.

For over 400 days, Rawan endured the brutality of genocide, bearing the weight of siege and bombardment without losing her strength or smile.

On November 21, 2024, Rawan was martyred in a treacherous attack. She was not alone; her older sister and younger brother also fell alongside her.

Though "Al-Rawana" is gone, she left us lessons in patience, strength, and love. She was an example of ambition despite adversity, and her memory will forever live in our hearts and minds.

Documented Her Cousin's Daughter

Date of Writing the Story: 2025/06/01

Umm Khaled Kullab

Mustafa was not just my husband, he was the pillar of my life and the light of my eyes. A cheerful man with a constant smile, he laughed through life's burdens and sorrows. His heart was vast, filled with love and compassion, and he cherished his siblings and family deeply.

We married, dreaming of building a quiet life together. Allah blessed us with two children who are my joy and soul. He was a dutiful son to his parents and steadfast in his faith, maintaining his prayers and devotion even in the toughest times.

Life wasn't easy for us. His brother, sister-in-law, and their children were martyred, and his nieces were injured. Yet, Mustafa bore all this with patience and gratitude to Allah's will.

Before his final departure, he bid farewell to his mother, kissed her, and said goodbye to me and our children, as if sensing it might be the last time. He left for treatment, and I waited for his return, but destiny was faster, he was martyred on his way back home.

He was more than a husband; he was a model of good character, known and loved in mosques and the neighborhood. Despite his pain, he never neglected his duties and exemplified patience and contentment.

Now, as Umm Khaled, I carry the pain of loss alone, raising my children while trying to be both mother and father to them. I often remember Mustafa's sweet smile and kind heart, which knew no hatred.

Life has been hard, but his love and patience have been my strength to face everything.

Date of Writing the Story: 2025/06/01

Manar Mahmoud Azzam

Age: 20 years

Manar was more than a friend, she was a sister and a soulmate who shared everything with me.

She was a devoted worshipper, her heart full of faith, and her melodious voice recited the Quran everywhere she went. We spent nearly every moment together, preparing ourselves to walk the path toward Allah's paradise. This was a sacred promise between us.

Manar was ambitious, generous, devout, and always eager to do good. Her beauty wasn't just in her appearance but in her noble character and refined manners.

I remember our last conversation. With a voice full of pain and need, she said, "I'm hungry, just one bite to fill my stomach." She wasn't speaking only for herself but expressing the suffering we all endured.

Manar, her husband, and child were martyred in northern Gaza during the first suhoor of Ramadan. Though her spirit departed, it remains with us. In her honor, I launched a Quran memorization project, fulfilling the promise we made together.

Manar was an everlasting light, and her voice and presence will forever linger in my heart.

Documented   Her   Friend
Date of Writing the Story: 2025/06/01

Umm Ayham Ajjour

Original Place: Tel Al-Hawa

My husband, Mohannad, was a kind-hearted man with a warm smile and beautiful eyes that adored our children, Mohammad and Ayham. He always prioritized our comfort, striving to provide us a dignified life despite Gaza's challenges.

One day, Mohannad went out to buy some necessities for our children. I never imagined it would be the last time I'd see him. The news of his martyrdom struck me like lightning. I wasn't prepared, and my heart couldn't bear this sudden separation.

He left me alone with our two young children, fighting every moment to explain to them that their father wouldn't return, though he is now in a better place. My pain refuses to subside.

Mohannad was my support, companion, and beloved. Losing him created a void in my life; the world feels darker without his laughter and embrace.

I pray to Allah for patience and strength to continue for his sake and our children's, asking Him to protect and safeguard them from harm.

Date of Writing the Story: 2025/06/01

Malak Al-Husari

Malak was not just a girl, she was a gentle presence that moved through life lightly yet left an unforgettable mark. Her voice was soft, but her words carried depth. Even in silence, her gaze spoke volumes, and her smile reassured troubled hearts.

At fifteen, she memorized the Quran, cherishing it as the soul clings to the body. She understood its teachings and lovingly advised those around her, not from a pulpit but from a sincere heart seeking guidance rather than imposing it.

Her friend Darin described her:"Malak was an angel. She left sweet imprints on everyone's lives. Quiet, exceedingly kind, with a beautiful soul and radiant smile. She stood by her friends and offered advice rooted in religion when needed. She impacted each of us profoundly."

Malak wasn't only a Quran memorizer, she was also a writer. She loved language, phrases, and immersed herself in texts like the sun melting into the sea at sunset.

Her writings seemed preparatory for absence, as if every sentence was a small farewell. One evening, she wrote:"If I'm ever absent and news fades... Remember, prayer is the bond between us."

She didn't know how soon her absence would come, nor that her words would be read after her passing, when memories become more precious than existence itself.

On the day of her martyrdom, her mother left to fetch flour for baking, leaving Malak and her siblings at home. But the flour never arrived, and the family was never the same again.

When her mother returned, there was no house, no sound, no children, only rubble, shock, and immense loss. Malak, her family, and most of her siblings were gone. Only her mother and one sibling survived, carrying this unbearable pain in fragile hearts.

Malak no longer sits beside her mother after Maghrib to review the Quran, no longer writes in her notebooks, and no longer says, "I write to leave a mark."

But she truly left a mark. Those who read her words pray for her without knowing her. Those who see her mother feel that mothers should never lose their children so cruelly.

Malak was a symbol of life, innocence, and serene faith. Though she is gone, she remains present in our hearts, pure, light, and luminous as ever.

Documented Her Friend, Dareen

Date of Writing the Story: 2025/06/01

Yumna Osama Al-Qirnawi

Age: 16 years

When I think of Yumna, I don't recall tragedies first, I see her smiling. Her pure face, green eyes like an untouched spring, and laughter that lit up spaces silently.

Yumna was close to me, closer than a soul in distressing times. We were inseparable, studying together, memorizing the Quran, dreaming, and sketching a future with childish imagination despite harsh realities.

At sixteen, she completed memorizing the Quran. She didn't stop at memorization, she understood, taught, and guided others toward enlightenment.

She reviewed and encouraged us, like a little mother caring for us with tender eyes and a big heart. Everyone who knew her loved her, for her noble character, filial piety, humility, and kindness evident even in her gaze.

One evening, shortly before her martyrdom, we spoke about life, ambitions, and the war stealing our peace day by day. Smiling shyly, she said: "I'm not afraid of death, but I hope I'm ready if it comes suddenly."

I didn't realize how close death was to her. On an ordinary day under war's shadow, a shell ended her existence and shattered her dreams. In an instant, Yumna was gone.

She was martyred on January 2, 2024.

All that remains of Yumna are her memories…And her voice echoing in my mind:"Oh Allah, make me among Your Book's guardians and Your chosen ones."

Her green eyes still linger in my thoughts, her scent fills empty spaces, and copies of the Quran mourn her. Friends miss her voice, conversations, and laughter.

You're gone, yet you haven't left our hearts. You were a flower in a time of ashes, and you've bloomed in paradise, where there are no shells, no pain, and no parting.

Date of Writing the Story: 2025/06/01

Tala Nader Abu Naji

Age: 15 years

How can I write about you, Tala, when you're not just a name in my memory, you're a piece of my soul, an unfinished line in my life?

As I write now, tears stream down my cheeks. I search through your messages, your voice, your laughter that still echoes in my ears whenever silence prevails.

Tala...
Fifteen springs and a bit more, you came and left in the same month you were born, completing a full circle. It's as if you came only to fulfill your mission, and then departed.

Tala was delicate to the point that you feared hurting her with a word. She loved her mother and siblings fiercely, cared for the young, respected the old, and nurtured her friends like a mother to them all.

She laughed, yes, but sometimes she felt something awaited her. Occasionally, she'd say with a mysterious look:"Rim, I feel like I won't live long... but I want to die a martyr, and I want my blood to mean something."

I'd gently scold her, saying, "Enough pessimism, you're still so young."She'd laugh and reply, "I love you, Rim, don't forget me."

A moment I'll never forget...One Ramadan night, we prepared suhoor under the dim light of a single candle due to power outages. Tala whispered as she placed a piece of bread in a small bag:"This is for Maryam next door. Her mother is sick, her father was martyred, and they have no food."

I asked, "What about you? Don't you have enough?"She smiled and said: "If we go hungry, we can wait. But Maryam is young... she doesn't know how to wait."

That moment stays with me. Tala thought of others more than herself, even in hunger and despair, always giving without expecting anything in return.

In her final message, she wrote:"Rim, take care of yourself. Allah willing, He won't harm any of us, and we'll meet again. Remember, I'll always love you."

I didn't know that message would be her last. Now, I search for her voice, finding only emptiness, and cling to memories of her smile and laughter whenever my pain deepens.

On October 25, 2023, Tala ascended as a martyr alongside her brothers Zakaria and Ahmad in a treacherous attack that left no trace of their dreams.

Tala…

You left behind indescribable pain, unforgettable memories, and an eternal imprint on our hearts. We'll remember you in every prayer, telling the world you were a remarkable person despite your short life.

I love you, Tala… And if we meet again in paradise, I'll never let you go.

Documented by Her Cousin

Date of Writing the Story: 2025/06/01

Umm Yusuf

Umm Yusuf... Between the Rubble and Mercy

I lived a simple life in the Al-Zeitoun neighborhood east of Gaza City with my husband and four children. Our house was modest, but it was filled with love, laughter, and the sound of the Quran that never left its corners.

On a Saturday morning, we heard the sound of explosions approaching. This wasn't unusual for us in Gaza, where planes never disappeared. But this time... the sound was different, closer, harsher, as if the earth itself was trembling. I grabbed my youngest son, Yusuf's hand, pressing his heart to calm his racing pulse. My husband shouted from afar: "Take the kids and head to the back street!"

We fled barefoot, taking nothing, no IDs, no food, not even a proper hijab. I covered my hair with an old kitchen cloth. We slipped through alleys and rubble. The cries of children here, remains there, and skies full of smoke. Midway,

I turned to look at my house, it was gone, reduced to a pile of stones. I collapsed, prostrated on the dust, and cried, not for the house, but for the memories, the Eid clothes I had saved for my children, and Yusuf's book.

We were displaced to a tent in KhanYounis, then to Deir al-Balah. Each day was harder than the last. No water, no medicine, no privacy.

At night, the girls would cry from the cold, and I would hold them while shivering myself. Sometimes, we ate nothing but dry bread and weak tea, if available.

But I didn't break down... I kept telling myself: "I will endure, not for me, but for them."

One day, a neighbor in the tent came to me and said: "There are children who don't know how to write; help them." I smiled for the first time in weeks. I had been a teacher before the war, and now I returned to teaching children with broken pens and torn notebooks, writing on sand. I wrote for them on cardboard:"Gaza does not die; it is reborn anew."

Today, after many long months, I am still in the tent. My face has changed, my back bent slightly, but my heart has grown stronger. I won't forget what I've lost, but I decided to be a small light in this darkness.

I am Umm Yusuf... a woman from Gaza.I was not defeated, despite everything.

Date of Writing the Story: 2025/06/01

Umm Mahmoud

Age: 42 years

Original Place: KhanYounis

My name is Umm Mahmoud, and I am 42 years old. Before the war, I lived a simple life in the Nuseirat Refugee Camp. My husband, "Abu Mahmoud," was a kind man who never raised his voice and always entered our home smiling. We weren't rich, but we were content with little, and we thanked Allah for it.

He worked in construction, and on some days he'd return drenched in sweat, carrying a bag of bread and some vegetables, jokingly saying to me: "Prepare the tea, O mother of the children, today we miss your gatherings." He never asked for much, only that his children were well and that he saw me smile.

Then the war came...

On the first day, they bombed our neighbors' house. Our home shook, glass shattered, and my children began to cry. I held them close and screamed: "Where are you, Abu Mahmoud?!"

He had gone out in the morning to buy milk for our youngest child... and never returned.

I waited for hours, convincing myself he would come back, perhaps hiding somewhere... but in the evening, our neighbor came, his face pale: "Umm Mahmoud, gather your strength... we found him."

My heart sank. I ran barefoot into the street... and found him wrapped in a white shroud.

I screamed, cried, prayed to Allah... then fell silent.

Everything inside me went dark, but when I looked at my three children, their eyes were fixed on me.

My middle son asked: "Mama, did Baba go to heaven?"

I nodded and said: "Yes, my love, he went to heaven, but we must keep pleasing him with our prayers."

The days passed heavily. We were forced to leave our home and flee. The only shelter we found was a ruined school. I placed pieces of cardboard under my children so they could sleep, and hid the youngest one's face in my chest to shield him from the cold.

For the first time in my life, I learned to be both a father and a mother.

I would go out searching for bread, returning with a tomato and a can of tuna, dividing it among the children, telling them: "The less food we have, the more blessings there are."

One night, Mahmoud, my eldest son, fell ill. I had no medicine, only warm water and frightened prayers.

I sat by his head, crying silently, whispering: "Where are you, Abu Mahmoud? I'm tired of doing this alone."

But he recovered... and smiled. He said to me: "I'm strong for you, Mama."

Date of Writing the Story: 2025/06/01

Umm Naser Abu al-Khayr

Age: 30 years

Original Place: Gaza

I was married to a man named "Saeed"... and his name truly fit him, filling our home with laughter and warmth despite our difficult circumstances.

We didn't own much, but we had a rare kind of love... and three children who were the light of my eyes: Naser, Youssef, and Mohammad.

On the first day of the war, Saeed went out to secure some supplies for us... and he told me:"If I don't return, take care of the kids... we only have each other."

I laughed that day and said to him:"Don't talk like that from the start... Allah will bring you back safely."

But he never came back.

In the evening, we heard an explosion near the market. My heart raced, and I called him dozens of times, but there was no answer... then the news came.

Saeed was martyred on the first day... the very first day!

It was as if he knew, as if he was saying goodbye when he said: "Take care of the kids…"

I froze, didn't scream, didn't cry... I just held Naser's hand, my eldest son, and pulled him close, as if trying to hide my face in him.

From that day on, everything changed.

I was no longer just a mother...

I became a father, a mother, a guardian, a teacher, a doctor, and a source of security for three children who didn't yet know how to live without the word "Dad."

We fled our home, leaving his picture hanging on the wall, and left with our clothes and some memories.

We now sleep in a tent, on the sand, and with every raindrop or gust of wind, I gather them in my arms and pillow my pain.

Youssef asks me every day:"Mama, when will Dad come back?" And I lie to him: "Dad is in heaven... and he's watching over us."

Then I go to a corner of the tent... and cry in silence.

Naser became the man of the house, helping me fetch water, standing in lines for bread or flour. Mohammad, the youngest, doesn't sleep unless he's in my lap, clutching my dress whenever he hears a plane, saying: "Mama, don't leave like Dad."

But despite everything... I haven't collapsed, and I haven't weakened.

Because I promised Saeed I would protect his children. And I promised myself I would plant hope in their faces, even if they are barefoot and hungry.

But I am a mother to three heroes, and I will remain steadfast... because I am not alone.

I am a woman from Gaza... and in Gaza, women do not lose.

Date of Writing the Story: 2025/06/01

Umm Saeed

Age: 56 years

Original Place: Shujaiya

Just two years ago, I lived a simple and peaceful life with my husband, "Abu Saeed," a kind man whose voice never rose in the house. He loved sitting with his children after Maghrib prayer, teaching and laughing with them. He always said to me:"I have a treasure... you and the children."

But suddenly... without warning, his heart stopped one dawn.

He left this world quietly, just as he had lived in it, and departed, leaving me with our only son, "Saeed," and a pain that still lingers in my chest to this day.

I cried a lot, but he always urged me to be strong and to raise Saeed with faith and manhood.

Saeed grew up quickly, as if he felt he had become "the man of the house." He read the Quran to me, brought me medicine, and always asked:"Are you pleased with me, Mom?"

And I would say:"You are all my satisfaction, Saeed."

Then the war came.

We fled our home to a tent in the south. Every night, I held him close as if he were still my little boy, even though he was a young man in his twenties.

One day, he said to me:"Mom, I must go help people... maybe I'll save someone, and maybe Allah will grant me a reward."

I said to him: "I'm scared for you, my love; you're all I have left."

He replied: "But I am Abu Saeed's son... and I don't run away from people's pain."

That night, we sat together in the tent under the dim light of a candle. He opened a small bag and took out a letter he had written to me, saying:"But if I don't return, Mom, don't cry too much... be proud of me."

He took my hand, placed it on his heart, and said:"Whenever you pray for me, your prayers will reach me; I'm sure of it."

He kissed my forehead, then left.

He went and never returned.

Saeed was martyred in the bombing while helping a family evacuate their children.

The news of his martyrdom reached me as I sat by the tent door... I brought his robe, smelled it, and cried like I had never cried before.

In just two years, I lost my husband and my son...

From a house full of laughter to a tent where the only sound is the groaning of a broken heart.

Today, I live alone.

All I have is a picture of "Abu Saeed" hung on the tent wall, Saeed's letter that I read every night and soak with my tears, and a small notebook where he wrote his dreams.

But despite everything I've been through, I stand tall...

I bake bread for the displaced, embrace children, and comfort widows like me.

Because I learned patience from "Abu Saeed" and courage from "Saeed"...

And because I am a woman from Gaza...

Where those who planted patience in their soil cannot be defeated.

Date of Writing the Story: 2025/06/01

Umm Khaled

Age: 60 years

My name is Umm Khaled, a widow for thirty years.

I lost my husband at a young age, leaving behind a small house and great hope in our hearts, me and our children. He was a strong man but didn't stay with us long. His sudden death left me responsible for raising five sons and three daughters. That day marked the beginning of a long journey of suffering and perseverance.

From that moment on, I became both mother and father to them.

I had no one to help me, so I worked tirelessly, cleaning houses, washing clothes, selling goods in the market, all to provide even a modest meal for my children.

But life wasn't easy…

As they grew older, my children married and started their own lives, leaving me alone. This left me facing loss twice: the loss of my husband and the absence of my children around me.

On cold winter nights, I missed their voices and laughter, but I didn't blame them, they were seeking a better life, and I understood that. Over the years, a resilience I never knew before settled in my heart.

I taught myself how to live with loneliness, turning my tears into water that nourished my dream of staying strong for my children and grandchildren.

Then came the war…

The war shook the foundations of my life like an earthquake. Many homes in our area were destroyed, and I lost neighbors and loved ones. Tents became my shelter, and I saw frightened faces of children and women around me. I embraced them as I used to embrace my own children when they were little.

Those days were complex; I can't describe the depth of this pain.

Physically and emotionally drained, every day felt like a new battle. But I refused to let my tears reveal my weakness to others.

One night during the bombardment, the sound of explosions shook the tent. I sat on the ground, praying to Allah to protect my children scattered far from me and my grandchildren. I didn't sleep that night; only Allah's hand was my refuge.

Another time, I decided to help orphaned children by opening my old home to those who had lost their families. I became their mother, sister, and companion. In doing so, I found meaning in my life, living for them and feeling my tears fade whenever I saw them smile, even if just for a moment.

I know I'll never fully heal from losing my husband or the distance between me and my children. But today, as a mother, I see myself in the story of every resilient woman in Gaza, fighting despite her wounds and shining through the darkness.

In the face of sorrow, I plant hope… because Gaza does not die, and we do not surrender.

Date of Writing the Story: 2025/06/01

Umm Mus'ab

Original Place: Gaza

A widow for twenty-five years, my husband left me early in life, entrusting me with the responsibility of raising our children. Alone, I raised them, holding onto our home despite life's hardships, never neglecting to protect and care for my children.

Years passed, and my children grew up. One by one, they got married and became independent. Yet, I remained alone, steadfast despite all the sorrows.

When the last war began, our suffering intensified. Amidst the chaos, my son Mus'ab was arrested by Israeli forces.

The news was devastating. My heart couldn't bear losing another loved one after my husband. Days and nights passed without any word about him, I didn't know where he was or if I'd ever see him again.

Every day, I prayed to Allah to protect him and bring him back safely. Despite my pain and fear, I tried to stay strong for my other children.

Forty-five agonizing days passed, each feeling like hell in my heart. Still, I refused to give up or lose hope.

Finally, Mus'ab was released. Though deeply scarred physically and emotionally, he returned to our home.

Now, after his return, I try to rebuild his life and restore his hope while still enduring the horrors of war and protecting my family from further pain.

I am Umm Mus'ab, a resilient woman who has endured much but never lost faith. I continue to fight for my children and my home in Gaza.

Date of Writing the Story: 2025/06/01

Umm Mohammad

Original Place: KhanYounis

I am Umm Mohammad. I raised my son since he was a child playing in the alleys, running after his friends and dreaming of a brighter future. In his eyes, I saw the innocence of childhood, a love for life, and immense hope despite the pain surrounding us.

Mohammad grew up to be a young, ambitious man who loved his homeland deeply. He often told me, "Mother, I will stay here to protect our land and people." Though I feared for him, I was proud of his fearless heart.

When the war broke out, our lives turned into an endless nightmare. Each day brought painful news, and every night, my heart raced with worry for Mohammad.

One day, I received the news that froze my blood, he was martyred in a battle defending his people and land. I couldn't believe it; part of my soul seemed to vanish, and the world lost its color.

Despite my overwhelming grief, I resolved to be strong, for Mohammad, for my children, and for every mother who lost a piece of her heart.

Instead of drowning in tears, I transformed them into a beacon of light to guide others. I visited mothers of martyrs, offering words of comfort and strength, standing with them against injustice.

One day, as I sat in the courtyard remembering Mohammad, a small boy from the neighborhood approached me, trembling from cold and sadness. With wide eyes, he whispered, "Mother, will Mohammad come back someday?"

I couldn't hold back. I hugged him tightly as tears streamed down my face and said, "Mohammad lives in our hearts. He is with us in every moment and returns whenever we remember him and love one another."

That moment felt like a ray of light in the darkness of pain. I realized my sorrow wasn't mine alone, it belonged to every child who lost a parent and every mother who lost a child.

Since then, I vowed to be a refuge for every lonely child and grieving mother, sharing stories of hope and planting strength and patience in their hearts. Mohammad and our heroic children deserve nothing less than our loyalty.

On every anniversary of Mohammad's passing, I sit with his children and grandchildren, recounting his bravery and the love that filled our home.

Though he is gone, my heart still beats with love for him. My wish is for peace to prevail so no mother has to endure this pain.

I am Umm Mohammad, a woman who lost her beloved son but never lost faith, strength, or hope for a better tomorrow.

Date of Writing the Story: 2025/06/01

Umm Ahmad

Umm Ahmad was known in the neighborhood for her patience and strength despite everything she endured. She lost her husband many years ago, and Ahmad became her sole support. Raised with love and care, he grew into an ambitious young man dreaming of building a dignified life for his mother and siblings.

When the war erupted, Ahmad joined the volunteers, protecting the neighborhood and aiding the wounded. Umm Ahmad feared for him daily but understood he followed his conscience.

One day, the unimaginable happened, he was martyred in combat. It felt as though the ground beneath her feet had split open, halting her life at that moment.

Unable to cry, for her tears had dried long ago, her heart screamed in agony. Sitting amidst the ruins of her home, clutching his photograph, she whispered, "You are our star, my hero. We will always be proud of you, no matter how much time passes."

Despite her immense loss, she chose to persevere for her younger children, becoming both mother and father to them, instilling hope and strength.

She says, "I lost Ahmad, but his spirit lives within us. The war taught me that strength isn't in the body but in the heart that refuses to surrender."

Each day, she ventures to the market, carrying life's burdens, talking to neighbors, helping widows and orphans, striving to be a voice for the voiceless.

This is the story of Umm Ahmad, a woman from Gaza who taught us that patience amidst adversity is the highest form of courage.

Date of Writing the Story: 2025/06/01

Umm Abdullah

Age: 36 years

Umm Abdullah, a woman from Gaza, lost more in the recent war than any mother should bear. She lived with her husband and four children in a small house in the Shuja'iya neighborhood, where life was simple despite challenges.

With the outbreak of war, everything changed. Sounds of explosions filled the air, rockets struck their homes, and they were forced to flee repeatedly. On a dark night, while trying to calm her children, a bomb detonated nearby. In an instant, she lost her eldest son, Abdullah, who had been shielding his younger siblings.

Tears never left her eyes, yet she refused to let despair enter her heart. Holding her son's body, she broke the silence with poignant words: "My son, you left before seeing the world, but my soul is with you, and my heart will never forget your laughter or kindness."

Her pain wasn't just for Abdullah but also for how to face her younger children, now dependent solely on her. Days later, her husband was martyred too, leaving her alone in this shattered world.

Still, Umm Abdullah remained resolute. Without losing hope, she cared for her children with love and dedication, instilling strength despite the profound grief in her heart.

She would say, "Gaza endures because we endure. Our wounds aren't the end but the beginning of renewed patience and greater hope."

Every moment of pain bore witness to the strength of her spirit, proving that love is unbreakable, even in the darkest times.

Date of Writing the Story: 2025/06/01

Sanaa Ghazi Said Turk

I am a citizen of Gaza, once dreaming of a dignified life full of security and stability for myself and my six children. We never imagined such a war would come upon us.

From the first days of the war until now, we haven't rested for a single day. Every day has been filled with exhaustion and hardship, from displacement to displacement, place to place. For two years, we lived in tents, experiencing fatigue in all its forms.

I lost many relatives and friends, and the hardest loss was my daughter's husband in KhanYounis. Now, my daughter and her seven children rely on me, and Allah knows the struggles I face to feed them, especially under famine and siege. There's no food, drink, or medicine, particularly difficult for me as I suffer from high blood pressure, as does my husband.

We now live in one tent, me, my daughter, and my children, thirteen of us altogether. Life is unbearably hard.

Truly, our lives are indescribable, bitter, tasteless, and colorless.

What is lost cannot return, my house, my work, even my memories.

Everything is gone, and we have nothing left, but praise be to Allah for everything.

Date of Writing the Story: 2025/06/06

Iman Fathi Kishko

The criminal Israeli forces bombed our home and obliterated our entire neighborhood. By some miracle, we escaped from the rubble as shrapnel flew and white dust enveloped everything. We fled without knowing where to go, our bodies exhausted.

Now homeless, we have no income, no food, no drink, and no aid reaches us, not even flour or money to buy anything.

Our situation is dire. My husband lost his job when the workshop he worked in was completely destroyed, and he can barely walk anymore.

We live in utter despair, awaiting death at any moment.

Our children are scattered everywhere, homeless and unemployed.

Even social solidarity has vanished.

We've lost everything due to destruction, bombings, hunger, and thirst.

No one defends us, and we take nothing from anyone…

Date of Writing the Story: 2025/06/06

Israa Hossam Al-Saudi

I am Israa, a 30-year-old Palestinian woman. Though my age may seem ordinary, I often feel as though my years are doubled, for I have endured what even mountains would struggle to bear—loss, hope, breakdowns, and resilience.

My story began when I was just a little girl. In 2006, my father, the martyr Hossam Al-Saudi, was taken from us by a treacherous shell fired by the occupation forces. I was his eldest daughter, his spoiled princess, and my mother's companion and helping hand after his passing. At such a young age, I learned the meaning of orphanhood—celebrating holidays without a father, walking through life without support, and laughing with a piece always missing.

Despite this profound loss, my mother never broke. She taught us to persevere, to become something great, just as our father had dreamed for us. Thanks to her strength, we grew into accomplished individuals: a doctor, an engineer, a translator, and another engineer. As for me, I became a passionate teacher who loved education.

In 2014, I married "Fareed," a noble man who became my new pillar after the one I lost. Together, we embarked on life's journey, but our first test came swiftly with the war of 2014. We were displaced, and stability shattered. Yet, amidst the chaos, I was blessed with my angelic daughter, Lama, who adored poetry and painting and brimmed with kindness.

Then came May in 2016, with her golden voice singing anthems for Palestine, followed by Huda in 2019, who lit up my life with her recitations of the Quran and poetic words that flowed like those of a little bard.

In 2020, my family contracted COVID-19, and we were quarantined at "Blue Beach" on Gaza's shore. It was during that isolation that inspiration struck—an idea for a home-based chocolate business. With no prior experience but immense determination, we bought a few molds and ingredients and started experimenting. The first sweet pieces were crafted in my kitchen, shared with my family, and they loved them. "Start a project, Israa," they encouraged.

I hesitated. For seven years, I had been a beloved teacher at the Malaysian School. I was successful, passionate about my work, and responsible for my three daughters, my mother, and our home. How could I balance it all? But eventually, I decided to take the leap.

I launched my project, creating sugar-free chocolates using stevia for diabetic patients, and participated in my first exhibition in 2021. My booth was among the most successful, earning me a three-month contract and opportunities to grow my venture.

I faced a crossroads: teaching or my business? I chose my new path. Leaving behind my teaching career, I dedicated myself fully to my factory. Slowly, my story spread. Local and international journalists visited me, writing beautiful stories about my journey. My small company began supplying major stores across Gaza. Through my work, I supported seven families while Fareed stood steadfast as my partner in success.

In 2023, I hosted my finest exhibition yet at the Social Development Building. Every detail, down to the packaging, bore my personal touch. But alas, war once again knocked on our door, stealing everything from me.

Acknowledgment and Gratitude

Words race against one another, and phrases jostle for space, striving to weave a garland of gratitude worthy only of you.

To you, those who penned the letters with the tears of your hearts and the anguish of your memories, to you who spoke the truth of the story without awaiting reward.

To you, we dedicate these words of thanks and appreciation. To the luminous vision and forefront that carried the burdens of women in "Women in the Hell of War". You surpassed mere documentation, creating instead a human project that gathers stories like scattered pieces of a broken mirror, reflecting education amidst the pain of Gaza – the wounded land – under the senseless war waged on our people.

I remembered you as a white dove, fluttering its wings, soothing the sorrow within us...

For the first time, I was able to write the sacredness of feeling.
And to the esteemed teachers who played a significant role in bringing this noble work to light, as well as the experts and educational supervisors:

Dr. Maisa Youssef Helles
Dr. Zahir Al-Banna

And to the bearer of triumph and enlightened ideas, who gathered spirits and pens, printing them with love and sincerity... illuminating the very letters with what her heart carries, she who has lived through the war and tasted its bitterness. We never needed a living heart or witness more than now, for how beautiful it is when a person becomes a candle, lighting the paths of others...

~Dr. Zahir Al-Banna of the Arab Heritage House, Canada

Also gratefully acknowledged for their invaluable assistance with editing and translating:

Dr. Maysa Yousef Abdlla Helles
Dr. Zaher Mohammed Abu Jubbah
Shaima Khalil Mohammed Abu Jubbah
Ismail Al-Wahidi

www.ingramcontent.com/pod-product-compliance
Lightning Source LLC
Chambersburg PA
CBHW070547130626
46556CB00001B/57

* 9 7 9 8 9 9 9 2 5 6 8 3 6 *